The Atari Assembler

The Atari Assembler

Don Inman   Kurt Inman

Reston Publishing Company, Inc.
A Prentice-Hall Company
Reston, Virginia

ISBN 0-8359-0237-4
ISBN 0-8359-0236-6 pbk.

Contents

Illustrations

Preface

Due to the spectacular growth of the use of personal microcomputers such as the Atari 400 and 800 models, more and more people are acquiring their own computers. These new users naturally want to make the most of the capabilities of this versatile tool. After conquering BASIC language, an assembler is the next logical step.

The Atari Assembler Cartridge provides the ideal tool. It is powerful, and yet simple to understand and use. It provides all the features necessary to take the drudgery out of hand assembling machine language programs.

We have written this book with two main objectives in mind:
  (1) to provide simple, detailed directions for using the Atari Assembler Cartridge;
  (2) to provide fundamental information on programming in assembly language.

The book is written for the beginning assembly language programmer who has some knowledge of BASIC language programming. Steps for using the assembler are given in detail. Sketches of the video screen are shown at intermediate and final stages for entry and execution of programs. Machine language instructions are explained both verbally and pictorially. Every effort has been made to make the book easy to read and understand.

We believe the approach to assembly language programming through BASIC is sound. We assume you have a knowledge of BASIC, and we try to ease you gently into assembly language using your existing knowledge of BASIC.

Chapter exercises and answers are given to reinforce what you have learned. Although the book is not meant to cover the Atari Assembler Cartridge or the 6502 instruction set completely, it provides enough detail to allow you to use both at an intelligent level. From that point, you are encouraged to use what you have learned to explore assembly language to the depth that you desire.

Chapter 1

Introduction

This book is primarily concerned with the operation and use of the Atari Assembler Cartridge. The Assembler Cartridge plugs into the left slot of the Atari computer replacing the BASIC language cartridge.

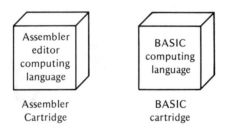

Assembler   BASIC
Cartridge   cartridge

Figure 1-1. Language Cartridges

Through the Assembler Cartridge programs, an assembly language program is written and edited. It is assembled into machine lanaguage codes, and the machine language program is then executed to produce the desired results. The steps in this procedure are outlined in Figure 1-2.

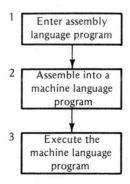

Figure 1-2. Steps in Assembly Language Programming

Our discussion of the Assembler Cartridge and its use will begin in Chapter 4. Instead of jumping right into the cold waters of assembly language programming, you should try a more gentle approach. In this chapter and the next, you will learn about the Atari's organization (or architecture) and go through a quick review of its BASIC language, with which we assume you are familiar. You will learn to create and execute machine language programs from within a BASIC program of your own in Chapters 2 and 3 (see Figure 1-3). We are using this approach because most users of the Model 400 and 800 Atari computers will probably do most of their programming in the Atari BASIC language supplied in cartridge form with their computers. This will allow you to learn the fundamentals of machine language programming through a language with which you are already familiar.

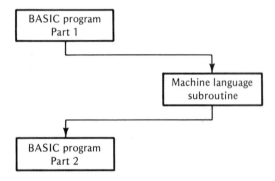

Figure 1-3. Machine Language Subroutine from BASIC

BASIC language instructions must be translated or interpreted (by the BASIC language cartridge) before the computer can understand what is to be done. Because of this extra step for translation, instructions in BASIC cannot be executed as quickly as instructions written in machine language. A program written in BASIC also uses more memory space than the equivalent program written in machine language.

It is possible to write most of a program in BASIC and write parts that must be done quickly and efficiently in machine language. The machine language parts of the program are accessed as subroutines from the BASIC program. These subroutines can be "understood" directly by the computer, and no time is wasted for interpretation. Chapters 2 and 3 will thoroughly explain this method and provide sample demonstrations and step-by-step instructions.

Although the computer can execute machine language instructions faster than it can execute BASIC instructions, it takes the programmer longer to write a machine language program.

There are several disadvantages to machine language:

1. Each instruction has its own *numeric* code which the computer understands. The programmer must either memorize these codes (Heaven forbid!) or look them up in a table each time they are used:

Examples:

Hex Code	*Operation Performed*
A9	Load the accumulator with the number following the hex code.
AD	Load the accumulator with the number contained in the memory location that follows the hex code.
8D	Store the value in the accumulator into the memory location that follows the hex code.

2. Each machine language Operation Code (Op Code) must be placed in memory in the correct sequence for the successful operation of the program.

3. When branches are made to change the sequential operation of a program, the programmer must calculate and include in the instruction exactly how many memory locations must be skipped to arrive at the correct instruction.

4. The detail work involved in machine language programming is tremendous, and the chance for programming errors is very high.

Assembly language eliminates many of the drawbacks of machine language programming. Compare the following list to the disadvantages of machine language.

1. Each assembly language instruction has its own *mnemonic* code which is an abbreviation of the operation to be performed.

Examples:

Mnemonic Code	*Operand*	*Operation Performed*
LDA	#14	Load the accumulator with the number 14.
LDA	$1100	Load the accumulator with the value contained in memory location 1100.
STA	$1105	Store the value contained in the accumulator in memory location 1105.

These mnemonic codes are much easier for a programmer to work with than the numeric codes of machine language.

2. The assembly language program has line numbers similar to BASIC, and the program is automatically placed into the correct sequence of memory locations by the assembler.

3. Through the use of labels (combinations of words, letters and/or numbers) branches are made to labeled instructions, and no calculations are required (the assembler does it for you).

4. The assembler creates the machine language program for you from the mnemonic codes, eliminating all the time-consuming detail work. The chance for programming errors is much less than for programs constructed by hand in machine language.

The Atari Assembler Cartridge will be introduced in Chapter 4 after you learn a little more about how the computer works in its own language.

COMPUTER ARCHITECTURE

We assume that you are familiar with your Atari BASIC programming language and now wish to investigate the computer's capabilities through its own language.

Programming in the machine's language requires that you become familiar with the fundamental building blocks (or architecture) of the Atari computer. The two building blocks that you will be most concerned with are the Central Processing Unit and the computer's memory.

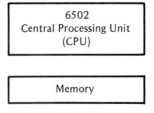

Figure 1-4. Atari Building Blocks

You will need an understanding of how the computer's memory is used for storage and retrieval of information. You will get to know the binary codes used to "instruct" the computer. These codes are referred to as the *instruction set* of the Central Processing Unit.

It sounds very complicated, but we will move slowly. One thing will be introduced at a time, and we will repeat previously discussed information at frequent intervals.

The Atari 400 and 800 model computers use a Central Processing Unit (CPU) called the 6502. The 6502 is a member of a family of microprocessors developed by MOS Technology, Inc., the MCS650X product family. This CPU can process, or execute, a set of instructions (listed in Appendix A) that are identified by their machine language codes. The codes are composed of binary numbers that are 8 binary digits (bits) long.

Binary digits come in two denominations. A binary digit is either a 1 (one) or a 0 (zero). A machine language code which can be recognized by the 6502 CPU is made up of 8 of these binary digits.

Examples:

Binary code	*Instruction*
10101001	Load the accumulator with the number following this instruction.
10101101	Load the accumulator from the memory location that follows this instruction.
10001101	Store the value that is in the accumulator in the memory location that follows this instruction.

Note that each code is exactly 8 binary digits (8 bits) long. The block of 8 bits is called a *byte*. The accumulator, mentioned in the instruction, is a special storage location called a *register*. It can hold one byte of data at a time.

The accumulator (often referred to as register A) is probably the busiest register (a special temporary storage location) in the system. All operations between memory locations must be communicated through the accumulator or one of the other registers. The accumulator is used as a temporary storage when moving data from one memory location to another. Operations on data are performed in the accumulator. Therefore, it is used in many of the machine language and assembly language instructions. It "accumulates" the results of successive operations on data as the instructions request.

It is convenient for a programmer to think of the 6502 microprocessor as consisting of several functional elements. Figure 1-5 shows the registers (special storage locations within the CPU) that are used repeatedly as the computer performs its many and varied chores. Some of these elements are used for specific purposes, and others are used for general purposes as needed by the programmer.

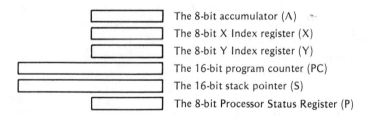

The 8-bit accumulator (A)

The 8-bit X Index register (X)

The 8-bit Y Index register (Y)

The 16-bit program counter (PC)

The 16-bit stack pointer (S)

The 8-bit Processor Status Register (P)

Figure 1-5. 6502 Functional Elements

Data is transferred between memory and the processor's internal registers over 8 bidirectional data lines called the *data bus*. Each bit of a data byte passes along its own line. However, the transfer of the whole byte (all 8 bits) of data takes place at the same time. Even though each bit travels along a separate path (line) of the data bus, the byte is transferred as one complete unit. Thus the structure of the 6502 microprocessor is said to be a byte-oriented structure. The 8 lines together are referred to as a bus.

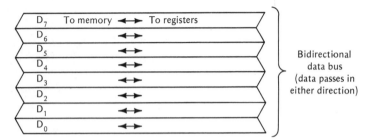

Figure 1-6. 8 Line Data Bus

The X and Y registers are also used for temporary data storage. In addition, they have the ability to be incremented and decremented by a programmed instruction. When the X or Y register is incremented, the value in the register is increased by one. When X or Y is decremented, the value in the register is decreased by one. Therefore, the X and Y registers can be used as counters (or pointers) to store data into successive memory locations or to load data from successive memory locations. This ability to point to successive memory locations is called *indexing* (hence their name: index registers). They can also be used as counters to determine conditions for ending a series of repeated operations (a loop). The 6502 instruction set includes several special instructions to load the index registers with predetermined values to facilitate the execution of loops in a manner similar to BASIC language FOR-NEXT loops.

The 16-bit program counter acts as a program address pointer to assure that instructions are executed in the desired order. Instructions of a program are stored in consecutive locations in memory. They are made up of machine language operation codes and/or address bytes and numbers to be operated on. To control the desired sequence of operations of a program, the program counter is used as a pointer to designate the position in memory where the microprocessor will obtain each successive instruction. The program counter is incremented, after each instruction is "fetched," to point at the next instruction to be performed.

	Memory location	Instruction or data
Program counter →	1000	A9
	1001	00
	1002	69
	1003	01
	1004	C9
	:	:

Figure 1-7. Program Counter

The stack is a special area of memory that is used to save data according to the sequence in which it is stored. It acts like a Last-In, First-Out file system (Figure 1-8). The 16-bit stack pointer keeps track of where data has been stored

Stack

Last on will be
the first off

Figure 1-8. Last-In, First-Out Stack

within the stack. It contains an address designating the current location of the *top* of the stack. The stack pointer and the program counter are large enough (16 bits) to hold a full-length address (0 through 65535).

Individual bits of the 8-bit Processor Status Register are used to keep track of specific effects that instructions have on the "status" of the computer. The presence or absence of an effect is shown by whether a particular bit has been *set* to one or *reset* to zero. These individual bits are also called *flags*. Flags used by the 6502 microprocessor are Carry, Zero, Interrupt, Decimal, Break, Overflow, and Negative. These conditions (or effects) are discussed in more detail as they are needed in understanding the instructions. Your first encounter will be with the Carry flag in Chapter 2.

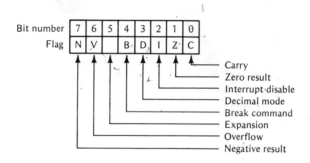

Figure 1-9. Processor Status Register

REVIEW OF BASIC

In Chapter 2, we will introduce the use of machine language programs that are entered through the use of BASIC language programs. The machine language program will be a subroutine of the BASIC program. Atari's BASIC includes a function that is used to transfer from the BASIC program to such a machine language subroutine. It is known as the *USR function.*

Example:

120 X = USR(1000)

Go to the machine language subroutine at memory location 1000

The balance of this chapter is devoted to the review of some of the BASIC statements, commands, functions, and keywords used by the Atari 400/800 computers. Special attention should be given to the USR function as well as the POKE, PEEK, and ADR keywords. If you feel the review unnecessary, proceed to Chapter 2.

Atari BASIC uses statements and keywords that are different from other BASIC language versions due to the computer's special graphics and sound capabilities. These are briefly described here. For more complete descriptions refer to the Atari BASIC Reference Manual.

Graphics Keywords

COLOR Primarily selects the appropriate color register, but specific uses depend on the graphics mode in use.

DRAWTO Draws a line from a PLOTted point to the point specified.

FILL Not really a keyword but an I/O operation that fills an area on the screen between plotted points and lines with a specified color.

GET Used to input the code byte for the character displayed at the cursor location.

GRAPHICS Controls which graphics mode is to be used.

LOCATE Stores the color number that controls a particular point on the screen in the specified variable.

PLOT Plots a point in the graphics window based on the X,Y coordinates specified.

POSITION Places the cursor at a particular location on the screen.

PUT Used to output data to the screen for display.

SETCOLOR Sets the color register specified by loading it with the hue and luminance data specified.

Sound and Game Keywords

PADDLE Returns the status of the specified controller (a number between 1 and 228 depending on paddle position).

PTRIG Returns a number representing the status of the trigger button of a controller (0 if button pressed, otherwise 1).

SOUND Plays a note through one of four specified voices, with the pitch, distortion, and volume specified.

STICK Same function as PADDLE, but for joystick controllers.

STRIG Same function as PTRIG, but for joystick controllers.

Special Keywords

Four keywords that are of special importance to us are: ADR, PEEK, POKE, and USR. These words provide a link between BASIC and machine language programs.

ADR This function returns the memory address of a specified string. Knowing the address enables the programmer to pass data to USR subroutines. A two-step process is used to obtain the address of a matrix of numeric values. First use a DIM statement for a string of length 1. On a separate BASIC program line, ask for the address of the string variable.

Example:

200 DIM A$(1)

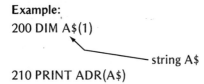 string A$

210 PRINT ADR(A$)

The address of the matrix will be one more than the address of the string A$.

The ADR function must be used with care. If your program (made up of the data matrix) is not addressed correctly, the computer may go off to Never-Never Land (the wrong place) and not return. If this happens, you can turn the computer off, wait about 5 seconds, and power up again. Your program will have gone bye-bye in the meantime. Start all over again.

PEEK This function allows the user to PEEK into a specified memory location. The user can then make use of the information that is "seen" there in his BASIC program.

Examples:

200 PRINT "THE LEFT MARGIN IS SET AT"; PEEK(82)

> This memory location always contains the position at which printing on the screen begins for each line (ordinarily 2).

210 PRINT " THE RIGHT MARGIN IS SET AT"; PEEK(83)

> This memory location contains the rightmost position at which a character is printed on the screen (ordinarily 39).

Any memory address (given in decimal form) in your Atari may be PEEKed at without disturbing its contents. This applies to either ROM (Read Only Memory) or RAM (Random Access Memory). RAM is the kind of memory that may be either written into or read from. ROM can only be read from. We will often use this instruction in Chapter 2 to PEEK at machine language programs that we have entered in memory.

POKE This function is the opposite of PEEK. You can use it to insert or modify the contents of RAM memory. We will use it in Chapter 2 to POKE in machine language programs.

Examples:

150 POKE 82,8

160 POKE 83,30

Change the left margin for screen printing to position 8

Change the right margin to 30

This would perform the following function.

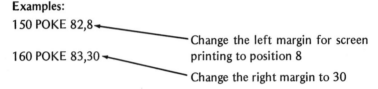

01234567890123456789012345678901 23456789 ← Screen
PRINTED MATTER ACCEPTED   positions
ONLY FROM POSITION 8-30   (0-39)

POKE, like PEEK, can be used in either the direct or deferred program mode. You *cannot* POKE data into ROM memory. Data can only be read from ROM, not written. Since a POKE statement actually changes data stored in memory, great care must be taken when using it. If incorrect data is POKEd into memory or if data is POKEd into the wrong memory location, disastrous results may occur. When you want to use POKE, refer to the Atari memory map in Appendix G of the Atari BASIC Reference Manual.

One precaution before indiscriminately using POKE. PEEK first and write down the value in that memory location into which you wish to POKE. Then, if the POKE doesn't produce the desired result, you can POKE the original value back where it was.

USR This function "calls" a 6502 machine language subroutine and returns with the result of the subroutine's execution. It will be used in Chapter 2 to execute the machine language programs that are POKEd into memory. The format used for this function is:

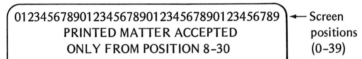

USR(X,Y,Z,. . . .)

An integer or   Optional input arguments
arithmetic expression   (variables that are passed
that evaluates to an   to the subroutine)
integer. It is the deci-
mal address of the be-
ginning of the machine
language program.

Definitions

The following definitions were condensed from the Atari BASIC Reference Manual for a quick review.

ARRAY   A list of places where items can be filed away for future use.

ARRAY VARIABLE   A name for an array consisting of one or more elements.

BASIC statement   Similar to a sentence in English; requests the computer to do something.

BREAK KEY   Pressed to stop a program's execution.

CONCATENATION   The joining of two or more strings.

CONSTANT   A number or string without a variable name.

DEFERRED PROGRAMS   Those stored in memory (with line numbers) for future execution.

DIRECT PROGRAMS   Those executed immediately as each line is entered from the keyboard.

EXPRESSION   May consist of any combination of legal variables, constants, operators, and functions used together.

FUNCTION   A computation built into the computer's operating system so that it can be used by the user in his programs.

KEYWORD   Any reserved word used by BASIC that *cannot* be used for other purposes.

LOGICAL LINE   Each numbered line in a BASIC program; consists of one to three physical video screen lines terminated by a RETURN.

NESTED LOOP   One loop (inner loop) executed within another (outer loop).

OPERATOR   Symbols used to perform operations such as arithmetic, comparison or logic.

RETURN KEY   Pressed to enter each program line.

STRINGS   A group of characters strung together with quotes.

VARIABLES   The name for a number or string.

For a complete list and discussion of Atari BASIC, refer to the Atari BASIC Reference Manual. With this brief review let's move right on to Chapter 2.

Chapter 2

Machine Language
from BASIC

Short machine language programs can be written and executed from BASIC through the use of the USR function. In this way, it is possible to execute part of a program in BASIC, "jump" to a machine language subprogram and then return to BASIC again. Figure 2-1 shows the flow of such a program.

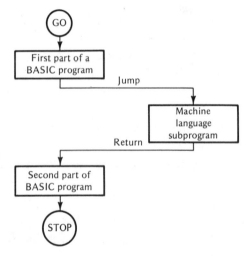

Figure 2-1. Program Flow Including Subroutine

The computer can only understand instruction codes written in fixed-length binary numbers. These binary instruction codes are called *machine language.*

BINARY NUMBER PATTERNS

The computer interprets these bits as being one of two numeric symbols, 0 or 1. The pattern of 1's and 0's makes a meaningful word, or a complete idea, to the computer. Therefore, we need to learn these words if we are to communicate directly with it.

An example of a pattern of 8 computer bits (a pattern with a size and shape that the computer can understand) is shown.

0   1   0   1   1   0   1   1
OFF ON OFF ON ON OFF ON ON

The computer would recognize this pattern as a unique number code and would respond by taking a specific action or using the number as a specific piece of data.

The Central Processing Unit (CPU) of the Atari computer was originally manufactured by MOS Technology, Inc. At the present time, two other companies (Synertek and Rockwell) also manufacture the CPU. This unit is named the 6502 microprocessor. It is called a Central Processing Unit because all instructions and numerical values are routed there for processing.

The 6502 microprocessor (and hence, the Atari computer), like many other microprocessors, only understands instructions which are coded in blocks of eight binary digits, called bytes. Therefore, the biggest hurdle to machine language programming is to learn to work with information in binary form.

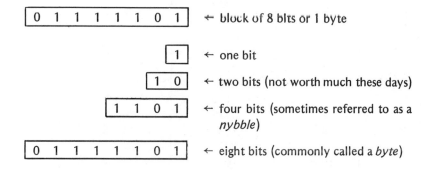

The Atari uses words that are eight bits in length, that is, it can digest words whose size is one byte. All instructions and numerical values must be sent to its *Central Processing Unit* in this byte size. A typical instruction, shown below, loads the computer's *accumulator* with the one byte of data following the instruction in a machine language program.

Load Accumulator from the L Register	
MNEMONIC CODE *(Abbreviation)*	*BINARY CODE*
LDA	1 0 1 0 1 0 0 1

Don't let the computer terminology throw you. The accumulator is similar to a memory location that is used in special ways which we will discuss later on. We are just introducing it here to show the format of an instruction.

The BASIC Language Cartridge, provided with your Atari, automatically interprets BASIC language statements and decimal numbers so that the computer can understand them. Therefore, when you are programming in BASIC, you enter decimal numbers and the results are displayed as decimal numbers even though the computer is working with binary numbers.

HEXADECIMAL NOTATION

Machine language codes are usually given in a third number system called *hexadecimal*. The hexadecimal system has a base of 16 and is used as a shorthand to represent binary numbers. Figure 2-2 shows a chart that demonstrates equivalent decimal, binary, and hexadecimal numbers.

Decimal	*Binary*	*Hexadecimal*
0	0000	0
1	0001	1
2	0010	2
3	0011	3
4	0100	4
5	0101	5
6	0110	6
7	0111	7
8	1000	8
9	1001	9
10	1010	A
11	1011	B
12	1100	C
13	1101	D
14	1110	E
15	1111	F

Figure 2-2. Decimal-Binary Hexadecimal Equivalents

We will often refer to this shorthand as hex. Four binary digits may be represented by one hex digit. Thus, our 8-bit instruction may be represented by a 2-digit hex number by breaking the byte (8 bits) into two parts.

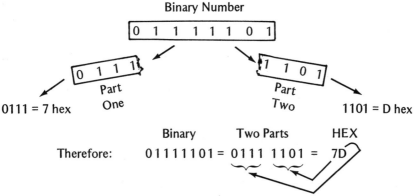

Binary Number

0 1 1 1 1 1 0 1

Part One   Part Two

0111 = 7 hex   1101 = D hex

	Binary	Two Parts	HEX
Therefore:	01111101 =	0111 1101 =	7D

Each place value in the binary system is a power of two, just as each place value in the decimal system is a power of ten. Two is called the *base* of the binary system, and ten is called the base of the decimal system. If we look at the place values of the binary numbers 0000 through 1111, we can attach more meaning to them.

Binary Places				Decimal Equivalent
2^3	2^2	2^1	2^0	
0	0	0	1	0+0+0+1 = 1
0	0	1	0	0+0+2+0 = 2
0	1	0	0	0+4+0+0 = 4
1	0	0	0	8+0+0+0 = 8

Using combinations of these place values, we may obtain any decimal value from 0 through 16 or any hex value from 0 through F.

Examples:

0101	=	$2^2 + 2^0$ = 4+1 = 5 decimal and also 5 hex
1001	=	$2^3 + 2^0$ = 8+1 = 9 decimal and also 9 hex
1100	=	$2^3 + 2^2$ = 8+4 = 12 decimal which is C hex
1011	=	$2^3 + 2^1 + 2^0$ = 8+2+1 = 11 decimal which is B hex

Let's now take a closer look at how we may express any 8-bit binary number by two hex digits. We saw earlier that the highest hex digit (F) corresponds to the four-bit binary value 1111. The next higher binary value is 10000. The one is in the 2^4 place which equals 16. Therefore, we have one 16 and nothing else. This can be expressed by the hex value 10, which means one 16 and no 1's. There is a direct relationship between upper 4 bits of an 8-bit binary number and the sixteen's place digit of a hex number.

| Binary Places | Hex value |
2^7 2^6 2^5 2^4	16^1
0 0 0 1	1
0 0 1 0	2
0 1 0 0	4
1 0 0 0	8

$2^4 = 16$
$2^5 = 2*16 = 32$
$2^6 = 4*16 = 64$
$2^7 = 8*16 = 128$

Next look at the binary place values of the complete 8-bit number.

| Binary Places | | | | | | | | Decimal Equivalent | Hex Equivalent |
2^7	2^6	2^5	2^4	2^3	2^2	2^1	2^0		
0	0	0	0	0	0	0	1	0+0+0+0+0+0+0+1 = 1	1
0	0	0	0	0	0	1	0	0+0+0+0+0+0+2+0 = 2	2
0	0	0	0	0	1	0	0	0+0+0+0+0+4+0+0 = 4	4
0	0	0	0	1	0	0	0	0+0+0+0+8+0+0+0 = 8	8
0	0	0	1	0	0	0	0	0+0+0+16+0+0+0+0 = 16	10
0	0	1	0	0	0	0	0	0+0+32+0+0+0+0+0 = 32	20
0	1	0	0	0	0	0	0	0+64+0+0+0+0+0+0 = 64	40
1	0	0	0	0	0	0	0	128+0+0+0+0+0+0+0 = 128	80

Figure 2-3. Eight-bit Conversion

Using combinations of all eight bits, you may obtain any decimal value from 0 through 255, or any hex value from 0 through FF. If we break an 8-bit binary number into two four-bit parts, each part may be represented by one hex digit.

Examples:

	Binary	01101101	64+32+8+4+1 = 109 in decimal
Split	binary	0110 1101	
	Hex	6 D	6*16+13 = 109 decimal
	Binary	11000101	128+64+4+1 = 197 in decimal
Split	binary	1100 0101	
	Hex	C 5	12*16+5 = 197 decimal
	Binary	10101100	128+32+8+4 = 172 in decimal
Split	binary	1010 1100	
	Hex	A C	10*16+12 = 172 decimal

HEXADECIMAL-TO-DECIMAL CONVERSION

Hex codes made up of one digit are quite easily converted to decimal values. If you haven't memorized the equivalents by now, here is a table of the values again.

Hexadecimal	Decimal
0	0
1	1
2	2
3	3
4	4
5	5
6	6
7	7
8	8
9	9
A	10
B	11
C	12
D	13
E	14
F	15

Figure 2-4. Hex Digit-to-Decimal Conversion

A two-digit hex code is also easily converted to its decimal equivalent if we keep in mind two things:

1. The decimal equivalent of each hex digit (as in the previous table).

2. The place value assigned to each hex digit.

Place values in the decimal number system are powers of ten. The least significant place in a decimal integer is valued at 10^0. This is called the one's place ($10^0=1$). The next place to the left is valued at 10^1 and is called the ten's place ($10^1=10$).

Examples:

$$89 = (8 \times 10^1) + (9 \times 10^0)$$
or
$$(8 \times 10) + (9 \times 1) = 80 + 9$$

digit   place   digit   place
    value   value

$$23 = (2 \times 10^1) + (3 \times 10^0)$$
or
$$(2 \times 10) + (3 \times 1) = 20 + 3$$

The hexadecimal place values are powers of sixteen (hexadecimal = 6 and 10). The least significant place in a hex integer is valued at 16^0. This is the one's place ($16^0=1$). The next place to the left is valued at 16^1 and is called the sixteen's place ($16^1=16$).

Examples:

23 hex = $(2 \times 16^1) + (3 \times 16^0)$

or

$(2 \times 16) + (3 \times 1) = 32 + 3$ decimal

= 35 decimal

digit   place
value   digit   place
value

89 hex = $(8 \times 16^1) + (9 \times 16^0)$

or

$(8 \times 16) + (9 \times 1) = 128 + 9$ decimal

= 137 decimal

A9 hex = $(10 \times 16^1) + (9 \times 16^0)$

or

$(10 \times 16) + (9 \times 1) = 160 + 9$ decimal

= 169 decimal

See if you can fill in the decimal equivalents of the following hex codes.

Hex Code	Decimal Equivalent
68	
18	
A9	
3F	
69	
41	
8D	
00	
18	
60	

Figure 2-5. Hex Code Conversion Exercise

If you have converted the hex codes of Figure 2-5 correctly, you are ready to enter your first machine language program. The codes are machine language instructions and data. Remember though, you are entering them from a BASIC program. Therefore, you must use the decimal form for entry. Check your answers now by looking at Figure 2-7.

Before the discussion of the machine language subroutine, let's take a look at the BASIC program used to enter and execute the subroutine.

BASIC PROGRAM—ADD TWO NUMBERS

```
100    REM INITIALIZE STORAGE ADDRESS
110    CLR: DIM E$(1), E(10)

120    REM POKE IN SUBROUTINE
130    FOR Y = 1 TO 10
140        INPUT N
150        POKE ADR(E$)+Y,N
160    NEXT Y

170    REM CALL SUBROUTINE
180    X=USR(ADR(E$)+1)

190    REM PRINT RESULTS
200    GR.0:PRINT "THE SUM IS ";
210    PRINT PEEK(6144)
220    END
```

Notice line 110. After the DIM statement for E$, it is necessary to dimension an array (E in this program) to the number of codes that are being used in the machine language program. This saves the necessary memory locations to receive the codes POKEd in by the FOR-NEXT loop in lines 130 through 160.

A flow diagram for the BASIC program and its machine language subroutine is shown in Figure 2-6.

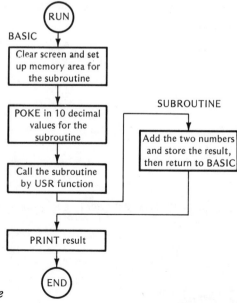

Figure 2-6. Flowchart
for Addition Subroutine

When you type RUN, the machine language subroutine is POKEd into memory. Each time through the input loop, enter one decimal equivalent of one hex code following the question mark (input prompt). The inputs are the decimal values that you put in Figure 2-5.

Hex Code	Decimal Equivalent	
68	104	
18	24	
A9	169	
3F	63 ◄	You are adding these
69	105	two decimal numbers
41	65 ◄	
8D	141	
00	0	
18	24	
60	96	

Figure 2-7. Decimal Equivalents of Hex Codes

After all 10 codes have been entered, the machine language subroutine is executed. On return from the subroutine the result is printed.

Enter the program and RUN it. This is the way it should look on the screen just before you press RETURN after the ninth input.

```
?104
?24
?169
?63
?105
?65
?141
?0
?24
?96              ◄─────────── The 10th input
```

After you press RETURN the tenth time, the screen is cleared and your result appears.

```
THE SUM IS 128
READY
■
```

Congratulations! You have just completed your first machine language program. When your BASIC program executed line 180, the USR function caused the execution of the machine language subroutine.

Figure 2-8 shows each hex code, the mnemonic code that will be used when you use Assembler language, and an explanation of the purpose of each code.

Hex Code	Mnemonic Code	Explanation
68	PLA	Pull one byte off the stack and place it in the accumulator
18	CLC	Clear the Carry flag
A9	LDA	Load the accumulator with the value immediately following
3F		Value loaded (3F hex = 63 decimal)
69	ADC	Add the hex value that follows to the value in the accumulator
41		Value added (41 hex = 65 decimal)
8D	STA	Store the value in the accumulator into the memory location that follows
00		Least Significant Byte of memory
18		Most Significant Byte of memory
60	RTS	Return from subroutine

Figure 2-8. Machine Language Subroutine

Notice that some codes consist of single bytes (68, 18, 60), some consist of two bytes (A9 and 3F, 69 and 41), and one consists of three bytes (8D and 00 and 18). Data and memory addresses accompany the appropriate instruction to form multi-byte instructions.

HOW THE MACHINE LANGUAGE PROGRAM WORKS

So far, we have said little about the the individual machine language codes. These codes have little or no meaning to you at this time, but each does have a precise meaning to the computer. Let's consider them in the following groups.

1. 68

2. 18

3. A9 3F

4. 69 41

5. 8D 00 18

6. 60

1. The first instruction (68) is the machine language code that tells the computer to pull one byte of data off the *stack* and place it in the accumulator.

The stack is a special area of memory where the computer keeps certain numbers and addresses in a specific order for later use. Each new item going onto the stack is placed on *top* of the stack. All other items are "pushed down" one place when a new item goes on top.

Example:

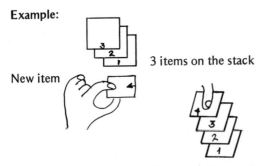

3 items on the stack

New item

New item is pushed on from the top.

When the USR function "calls" a machine language program from BASIC, the BASIC address to which the machine language is to return when done is placed on the stack in two separate bytes—low-address byte first, then high-address byte on top.

Top	yy	← High byte of return address
Bottom	xx	← Low byte of return address

The Stack

Following this, the computer puts any variables being passed to the machine language subroutine. The last item placed on the stack at this time is the number of variables that were passed. In our example, we didn't pass any variables. Therefore the stack looked like this when the machine language subroutine was called.

Top	0	← Number of variables passed
	yy	← High byte of return address
Bottom	xx	← Low byte of return address

In order to have the return address available when the subroutine has been completed, we had to remove that zero on top of the stack. So, we used the instruction (68) to pull the top value off the stack. It was placed in the accumulator by the instruction. The stack now has the return address on top ready for use.

Top   yy   — High byte of return address

Bottom   xx   — Low byte of return address

The Stack Now

0

The Accumulator Now

The number (0) in the accumulator will not be used, but we had to get it off the stack in order to access the return address bytes when needed.

     2. The second instruction (18) clears the Carry bit of the Processor Status Register (resets it to zero). The add instruction (fourth instruction) will automatically add the Carry bit when two numbers are summed. Since you do not want a carry to be added in, the instruction is used to ensure that the Carry bit is zero. Later, you will be doing some multiple-byte additions with larger numbers. At that time, you will see that the Carry bit must be used when adding all but the Least Significant Byte.

     3. The third instruction consists of two hex codes (or two bytes):

         A9 3F

A9 is the hex representation for the instruction, "Load the accumulator with the value that immediately follows." The 3F is the number that is loaded.

     4. The fourth instruction consists of the two hex codes (two bytes):

         69 41

69 is the hex representation for the instruction "Add the number that follows to the value in the accumulator." The result will replace the value in the accumulator. The hex value 41 is the number that is added.

     5. The fifth instruction consists of three hex codes (three bytes):

         8D 00 18

8D is the hex representation of the instruction, "Store the value that is in the accumulator into the memory location that follows." The memory location used is 1800 hex (6144 decimal). Notice that the memory location is too large to be expressed as one byte. Therefore, two hex codes are used. Notice also the order in which the high-address byte (18) and the low-address byte (0) are given. The low-address byte is first, followed by the high-address byte. This convention is followed when instructions contain a two-byte address.

     6. The last instruction consists of a single hex code (one byte):

         60

60 is the hex representation of the instruction, "Return from subroutine." This single instruction tells the computer to return to the place where it came from.

The computer takes the top two bytes off the stack in order to find where it should return in the BASIC program and obtain the next BASIC statement.

A machine language program is executed in sequential order by memory locations just as a BASIC program is executed by line numbers. There are exceptions like the BASIC GOTO and GOSUB statements. Machine language programs can perform similar tricks with JUMP and BRANCH instructions, as you will see later.

Although this book is mainly concerned with Assembly Language programming and the Atari Assembler Cartridge, you should realize that the computer actually works with machine language codes. The assembler language is merely an easier method to remember and enter machine language codes, as you will see in later chapters.

We have used six machine language instructions in this first program. Since machine language instructions are coded numbers, they are hard to remember. However, each one of them has a mnemonic code (an abbreviation for the meaning of the instruction) that is used in assembly language programming.

INSTRUCTIONS USED SO FAR

Machine Language Code	Assembler Mnemonic	Function
68	PLA	Pull one byte off the stack and place in the accumulator
18	CLC	Clear the Carry bit
A9	LDA	Load the accumulator with the hex value that follows
69	ADC	Add (with carry) the hex value that follows to the accumulator
8D	STA	Store the value in the accumulator into the memory location that follows
60	RTS	Return from the subroutine

SUMMARY

In this chapter, you have learned:

• To access a machine language subroutine from a BASIC program by the USR function of BASIC;

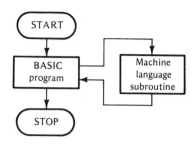

- That machine language instruction codes are binary numbers that can be entered in hexadecimal form;
- That some instruction codes occupy one byte, some two bytes, and some three bytes;
- How the "push down" stack is used to store numbers and addresses temporarily;
- How the numbers are pulled off the stack;
- That every machine language subroutine must have a Return from Subroutine instruction to send control back to the main program; and
- The following machine language instructions:

68	PLA	Pull one byte off the stack and place it in the accumulator
A9	LDA	Load the accumulator with the value immediately following
69	ADC	Add the hex value that follows to the value in the accumulator
8D	STA	Store the value in the accumulator into the memory location that follows
60	RTS	Return from Subroutine
18	CLC	Clear the Carry flag

EXERCISES

1. Hexadecimal codes are a short way to write _____ instruc-
   (decimal, binary)
   tion codes which the computer can understand.

2. What kind of numbers are used in BASIC language programs?
   _____
   (binary, hex, decimal)

3. Fill in the hexadecimal and decimal equivalents of the following binary numbers.

      (a) 1101 = _____ hex = _____ decimal

      (b) 0110 = _____ hex = _____ decimal

      (c) 10101001 = _____ hex = _____ decimal

4. When using a machine language subroutine from BASIC, you enter instruction codes in _____ form, and the BASIC interpreter converts them
                        (hex, decimal)

   to _____ form.
     (hex, decimal)

5. What is the three-letter abbreviation for the function used in Atari's BASIC to call a machine language subroutine?   ___ ___ ___

6. If you want to call a machine language program from BASIC and had dimensioned the variable E$ to 1 (100 DIM E$(1)) for this purpose, what is the BASIC line that would call the subroutine?

     500 _____

7. What is the last instruction that every machine language subroutine must execute to get back to the BASIC program?

     _____

8. Suppose you wish to store the decimal value, 72, in the memory location 1925 hex. The number 72 is now in the accumulator. The machine language instruction to store the value would consist of three bytes in the following order. Fill in the blanks.

     8D

     ___

     ___

9. In exercise 8, what hex value would be loaded into memory location 1925?

     _____

ANSWERS

1. Binary

2. Decimal

3. (a) 1101 = D hex = 13 decimal
   (b) 0110 = 6 hex = 6 decimal
   (c) 10101001 = A9 hex = 169 decimal

4. Hex
   Decimal

5. USR

6. 500 X = USR(ADR(E$)+1)

————————————————— This may be some other variable

7. 60 or RTS or Return from Subroutine

8. 8D
   25   (Don't forget the reverse order)
   19

9. 48   (4*16+8 = 72)

Chapter 3

Memory Use

When you use BASIC language and machine language programs together, you must use separate portions of memory for each language. Atari's BASIC interpreter (in the BASIC ROM Cartridge) takes care of allocating the memory locations used in the BASIC language part of your program. You must make sure that your machine language part uses a different area of memory.

ATARI MEMORY MAP

Certain areas of the computer's 65536 memory locations are used by the Atari Operating System (8K of ROM) and by the ROM cartridges (such as BASIC or Assembler) that may be plugged into the computer console. We cannot POKE machine language programs into these areas. The Operating System and ROM cartridges also use some of the system's RAM space. We must not POKE into those areas as we might destroy our own program or cause some other programming disaster.

Figure 3-1 shows a map of the Atari's memory. Look closely and you can see areas of memory called *Free RAM*. These areas may be safely used for your programs. However, as stated above, you must keep BASIC and machine language programs separated.

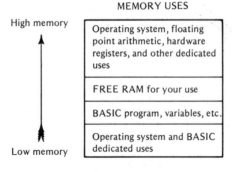

MEMORY USES

High memory

Operating system, floating point arithmetic, hardware registers, and other dedicated uses
FREE RAM for your use
BASIC program, variables, etc.
Operating system and BASIC dedicated uses

Low memory

Figure 3-1. Memory Map

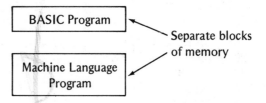

The technique which we have been using so far is to DIMension a string variable E$ to one (1). This saves one memory location immediately following the area used by our BASIC program. The address of this location will vary from program to program depending on the length of the BASIC program, but the machine language memory locations will always *follow* the BASIC program. We will demonstrate this with three short BASIC programs which are of different lengths. They all end by printing the address of the memory location saved for E$.

DEMO PROGRAM #1

```
10    CLR: DIM E$(1)
20    PRINT ADR(E$)
```

Enter and RUN Demo Program #1. You will see that one location was saved for E$ at address 11182.

```
RUN
11182

READY
■
```

DEMO PROGRAM #2

```
10    CLR: DIM E$(1)
20    FOR X = 1 TO 10    ← A very short time delay
30    NEXT X
40    PRINT ADR(E$)
```

Enter and RUN Demo Program #2. You will see that the location saved for E$ is now at address 11221. Since Demo Program #2 is longer than Demo Program #1, the location saved for E$ has a higher address.

```
RUN
11221

READY
■
```

DEMO PROGRAM #3

```
10    CLR: DIM E$(1)
20    FOR X = 1 TO 10
30        PRINT X;
40    NEXT X
50    PRINT
60    PRINT ADR(E$)
```

Enter and RUN Demo Program #3. You will see that the address saved for
E$ is higher yet because Demo Program #3 is longer than the other two.

```
.
.
.
RUN
12345678910
11235

READY
■
```

We have made use of the memory location saved for E$ to find a safe place
in RAM (out of the way of our BASIC program and other reserved areas) for our
machine language subroutines. We POKEd the machine language subroutine into
a memory area that started at the next higher location than that saved for E$.
We will continue to use this method.

HOW BASIC FINDS THE MACHINE LANGUAGE PROGRAM

You may wonder how your BASIC program knows where to find the machine language subroutine. Let's take another look at the program used in Chapter 2 that added two numbers.

First section

```
100    REM INITIALIZE STORAGE ADDRESS
110    CLR: DIM E$(1), E(10)
```

Save one memory ⟋   Save 10 locations for
location for E$ machine language subroutine

Second section

120	REM POKE IN SUBROUTINE	
130	FOR Y = 1 TO 10	
140	INPUT N	POKE 10 hex codes into
150	POKE ADR(E$)+Y,N	successive memory locations
160	NEXT Y	(E$+1 through E$+10)

Third section

170	REM CALL SUBROUTINE	Jump to the machine lan-
180	X = USR(ADR(E$)+1)	guage subroutine starting in
		memory at address (E$)+1

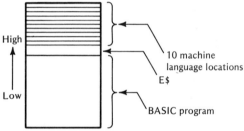

Figure 3-2. Memory Used for Machine Language Subroutine

The fourth section of the BASIC program prints the results of the machine language program.

Fourth section

190	REM PRINT RESULTS	
200	GR.O: PRINT "THE SUM IS";	← Print the label
210	PRINT PEEK (6144)	──── Print result that the machine
220	END	language program has placed
		in memory location 6144
		(1800 hex)

The computer saved one location for E$ in an area of memory that is out of the way of your BASIC program. At lines 130 through 160, the program POKEs the machine language codes into the memory just above the space that was saved for E$. Your BASIC program "calls" the machine language program at line 180 by the USR function. The USR function specifies the address where the machine language program can be found. Thus the USR function works like the BASIC statement: GOSUB

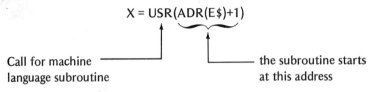

Call for machine language subroutine ——————

the subroutine starts at this address

The machine language hex codes are stored in memory as follows:

Memory Address	Hex code Stored
E$+1	68
E$+2	18
E$+3	A9
E$+4	3F
E$+5	69
E$+6	41
E$+7	8D
E$+8	00
E$+9	18
E$+10	60

Figure 3-3. Hex Code Storage

The Atari also has the capability of passing one or more quantities to a machine language program through the USR function.

Example:

100 A=5
110 X = USR(ADR(E$)+1,A)

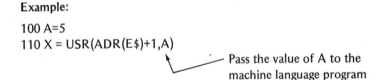

Pass the value of A to the machine language program

The value of variable A is palced on the stack as described in Chapter 2. The value is placed there as a two-byte hex number.

Let's review that process again:

1. The address to which the computer is to return in your BASIC program is placed on the stack.

yy	← High byte of return address
xx	← Low byte of return address

2. The value of variable A is placed on top of the stack. If A = 5,

00	← High byte of A
05	← Low byte of A
yy	← High byte of return address
xx	← Low byte of return address

3. The number of variables passed is placed on top of the stack.

01	← Number of variables passed
00	← High byte of A
05	← Low byte of A
yy	← High byte of return address
xx	← Low byte of return address

Your machine language program may then pull the values off the stack and use them.

PASSING VARIABLES TO MACHINE LANGUAGE SUBROUTINE

Following is an addition program that will demonstrate this methods. It allows you to input a value that is passed to the machine language subroutine. The value of five is added to your input by the machine language subroutine. The result is placed in memory so that the BASIC program can find it.

BASIC PROGRAM—ONE VARIABLE PASSED

```
100    CLR: DIME$(1), E(10)

200    FOR Y = 1 TO 10
210        INPUT N                  Input machine language
220        POKE ADR(E$)+Y,N         subroutine (10 bytes)
230    NEXT Y

300    GR.O: PRINT "INPUT A"        Input a positive decimal integer less
310    INPUT A                      than 251
320    X = USR(ADR(E$)+1,A)         Call subroutine
330    PRINT PEEK(6144)             Print sum of your number and 5
340    END
```

When the BASIC program is executed, the value of A will be placed on the stack, and your machine language program will pull it off and use it. The result will be printed when you come back to your BASIC program.

The following machine language subroutine shows the contents of the accumulator, memory storage location, and stack as the subroutine is executed.

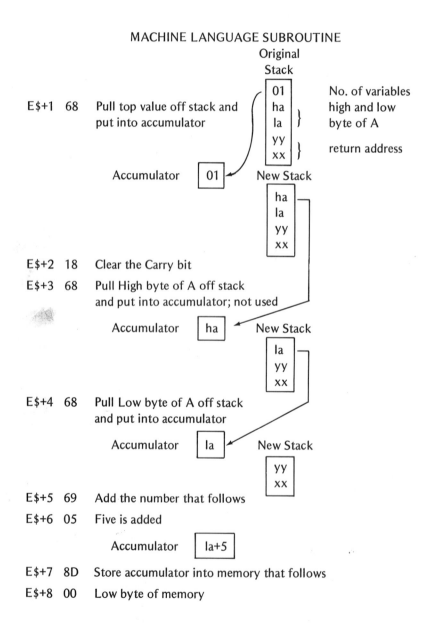

MACHINE LANGUAGE SUBROUTINE

E$+1 68 Pull top value off stack and put into accumulator

E$+2 18 Clear the Carry bit

E$+3 68 Pull High byte of A off stack and put into accumulator; not used

E$+4 68 Pull Low byte of A off stack and put into accumulator

E$+5 69 Add the number that follows

E$+6 05 Five is added

E$+7 8D Store accumulator into memory that follows

E$+8 00 Low byte of memory

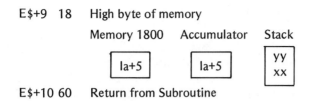

E$+9   18   High byte of memory

Memory 1800   Accumulator   Stack

E$+10 60   Return from Subroutine

USING THE ONE-VARIABLE PROGRAM

To enter and use the program, follow these steps.

1. Enter the BASIC PROGRAM—ONE VARIABLE PASSED.

2. RUN the BASIC program and ENTER these hex codes (one at a time in response to the ? prompt).

```
?104
?24
?104
?104
?105
?5
?141
?0
?24
?96
```

3. After the last entry, the screen will clear and the INPUT prompt will appear on the screen.

```
INPUT A?■
```

Try typing 95 and press the RETURN key.

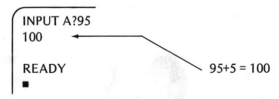

```
INPUT A?95
100
READY
■
```

95+5 = 100

You may try other numbers by typing GOTO 300 in response to the READY prompt. This will repeat step 3. Do not type RUN at this time or you will have to enter all the hex codes again as in step 2.

PASSING MORE THAN ONE VARIABLE

More than one variable can be passed from your BASIC program to your machine language subroutine by the USR function. The next program demonstrates this. It passes two variables, A and B. These two values are then summed by the machine language subroutine. Notice the changes in the BASIC program and the subroutine.

BASIC PROGRAM—TWO VARIABLES PASSED

```
100   CLR: DIM E$(1), E(16)              16 bytes this time

200   FOR Y = 1 TO 16
210        INPUT N                       POKE subroutine
220        POKE ADR(E$)+Y,N
230   NEXT Y

300   GR. O: PRINT "INPUT A";
310   INPUT A                            Two numbers input
320   PRINT "INPUT B";
330   INPUT B                            Both A and B put on
340   X=USR(ADR(E$)+1,B,A)               the stack
350   PRINT PEEK(6144)
360   PRINT "PRESS RETURN TO REPEAT";
370   INPUT A$:
380   GOTO 300                           Go back to try again
```

When line 340 is executed, the USR function causes the stack to be filled like this:

TOP	2	← Number of variables passed
	ha	← High byte of A
	la	← Low byte of A
	hb	← High byte of B
	lb	← Low byte of B
	yy	← High byte of return address
BOTTOM	xx	← Low byte of return address

Remember, when data items are pulled off the stack, they come off the top. The last item put on the stack is the first one taken off the stack. You may notice that two bytes are used for each number that was pushed on the stack.

When a two-byte number is used, one byte is referred to as the Least Significant Byte (LSB). The other is referred to as the Most Significant Byte (MSB).

Example:

MSB (Most Significant Byte)

2^7	2^6	2^5	2^4	2^3	2^2	2^1	2^0
1	0	0	0	1	0	0	1

LSB (Least Significant Byte)

2^7	2^6	2^5	2^4	2^3	2^2	2^1	2^0
0	1	0	0	0	1	1	1

Don't confuse the Most and Least Significant Bytes with the Most and Least Significant Bits. Each byte has an MSB (Most Significant Bit) and a LSB (Least Significant Bit).

MOST SIGNIFICANT BYTE

2^7	2^6	2^5	2^4	2^3	2^2	2^1	2^0
1	0	0	0	1	0	0	1

↑ most significant bit   ↑ least significant bit

LEAST SIGNIFICANT BYTE

2^7	2^6	2^5	2^4	2^3	2^2	2^1	2^0
0	1	0	0	0	1	1	1

↑ most significant bit   ↑ least significant bit

To use a two-byte number, you consider the Most Significant Byte as an extension of the Least Significant Byte. The place values of the Least Significant were assigned powers of two from 0 through 7.

LSB

2^7	2^6	2^5	2^4	2^3	2^2	2^1	2^0
0	1	0	0	0	1	1	0

= 64+4+2 = 70 (decimal)

The place values of the Most Significant Byte are assigned the next higher powers of two (8 through 15).

MSB

2^{15}	2^{14}	2^{13}	2^{12}	2^{11}	2^{10}	2^9	2^8
1	0	0	0	1	0	0	1

= 32768+2048+256 =
35072 (decimal)

The decimal value resulting from the combined bytes (considered as one number) is:

2^{15}	2^{14}	2^{13}	2^{12}	2^{11}	2^{10}	2^9	2^8	2^7	2^6	2^5	2^4	2^3	2^2	2^1	2^0
1	0	0	0	1	0	0	1	0	1	0	0	0	1	1	0

In decimal: 32768+2048+256+64+4+2 = 35142
Split into 4-bit parts:

```
          1000    1001    0100    0110  ←  This binary value
          ⌣       ⌣       ⌣       ⌣        is equivalent to
EX digits  8       9       4       6   ←  this hex value
```

Hex format:

MSB	LSB		16^3	16^2	16^1	16^0
89	46	=	8	9	4	6

→   8*4096 = 32768
+   9*256 = 2304
+   4* 16 =   64
+   6*1   =   6
                35142
           (decimal)

The use of two-byte numbers allows us to use larger inputs (up to 65535). However, our machine language program is only designed to add single-byte integers (0-255). Therefore, the High bytes of the variable A and the variable B are both zero. If you input numbers whose sum is larger than 255, you will get an incorrect result.

The machine language program is longer this time, consisting of 16 hex codes (16 bytes).

MACHINE LANGUAGE SUBROUTINE

Address	Hex Code	Function
E$+1	68	Pull top value off stack and store in accumulator
E$+2	18	Clear the Carry flag to prepare for addition of Low bytes of numbers
E$+3	68	Pull High byte of A and put in accumulator
E$+4	68	Pull Low byte of A and put in accumulator
E$+5	8D	Store low byte of A into memory location that follows
E$+6	01	Low byte of memory used for storage
E$+7	18	High byte of memory used for storage
E$+8	68	Pull High byte of B and put in accumulator
E$+9	68	Pull Low byte of B and put in accumulator
E$+10	6D	Add with carry the value in the accumulator and the value in the memory location that follows
E$+11	01	Low byte of memory
E$+12	18	High byte of memory
E$+13	8D	Store the result in the memory location that follows
E$+14	00	Low byte of memory used for storage
E$+15	18	High byte of memory used for storage
E$+16	60	Return from subroutine

Enter the BASIC program now and RUN it so that you can enter the machine language codes in the usual way. After the 16 hex codes have been entered, the screen clears and you will see the following.

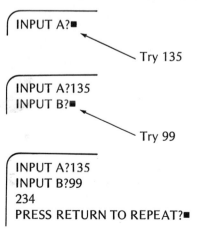

INPUT A?■

Try 135

INPUT A?135
INPUT B?■

Try 99

INPUT A?135
INPUT B?99
234
PRESS RETURN TO REPEAT?■

A new instruction is used at E$+10 of the **Two Variable** program. It is ADC (ADd with Carry) with a hex code of 6D. We used the hex code 69 for addition in earlier programs. Why the difference? Well, some of the functions, such as addition, can be performed in several modes. This will be more thoroughly discussed in Chapter 5. The 69 instruction adds the value immediately following it to the value in the accumulator. The 6D instruction adds the value that is contained in the memory location that follows the instruction to the value in the accumulator. Some instructions can be performed in only one mode, but others can be performed in more than one mode. Even though the instruction may perform the same function, each mode of the instruction performs the function in a different way. Therefore, each mode has a different hex code (called an Operation Code or Op Code for short) for each mode.

So far you have only seen machine language routines that proceed straight through consecutive memory locations. All of the arithmetic operations were performed in the accumulator, called the A register. The 6502 microprocessor has other registers which are used in different ways.

Since the computer is able to perform repetitive operations, such as a FOR-NEXT loop, in BASIC, you probably realize that similar operations can be done in machine language. In Chapter 1, a brief discussion of the X and Y index registers was given. Let's take a look now at how they can be used.

A MACHINE LANGUAGE LOOP

You have no doubt used FOR-NEXT loops many times in BASIC. In the next machine language subroutine, we'll utilize a similar looping technique using the X index register as a counter. Here is a comparison of the FOR-NEXT loop and a description of a machine language loop that would do about the same thing.

BASIC	MACHINE LANGUAGE
FOR X = 0 TO 9	Load X register with zero.
PRINT X	Store the value in the X register into memory.
NEXT X	Increment the X register.
	Compare the X register with 10.
loop	Branch back if X is not equal to 10.
	Return if X does equal 10.

The machine language program will be more detailed than the BASIC program. Each step must be implemented through exact machine language instructions.

Here is how the BASIC program and machine language subroutine will be accomplished.

FLOW OF BASIC PROGRAM

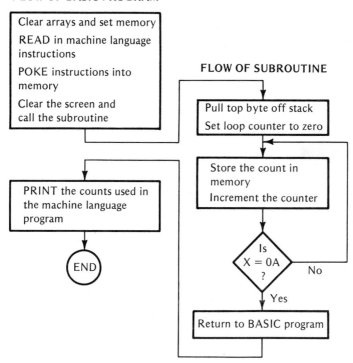

The hex codes for the machine language instructions are given in Appendixes A and B. A more complete description of the instructions can be found in the MCS6500 Microcomputer Family Programming Manual.* The instructions are listed by their mnemonic codes. The operation codes are given in hexadecimal form. Therefore, you need to convert them to decimal form in order to POKE them into memory from your BASIC program. Calculate the decimal equivalents for the machine language subroutine that follows. Fill in the blanks in the table.

---

*Published by MOS Technology, Inc., 950 Rittenhouse Road, Norristown, PA 19401.

MACHINE LANGUAGE SUBROUTINE

Address	Hex Code	Decimal equivalent	Mnemonic code	Comments
E$+1	68	_____	PLA	Pull byte off stack
E$+2	A2	_____	LDX 0	Load the X register with zero
E$+3	00	_____		
E$+4	8A	_____	TXA	Transfer the value in X register to the accumulator
E$+5	9D	_____	STA 1800,X	Store the value in accumulator into memory
E$+6	00	_____		
E$+7	18	_____		
E$+8	E8	_____	INX	Increment the count in the X register
E$+9	E0	_____	CPX 0A	Compare the value in X with 10 (decimal)
E$+10	0A	_____		
E$+11	D0	_____	BNE F7	Branch back if X = 10 (decimal) to address E$+4
E$+12	F7	_____		
E$+13	60	_____	RTS	Return from Subroutine

Figure 3-4. Machine Language Exercise

This subroutine uses several new instructions.

NEW INSTRUCTIONS USED

Six new instructions appeared in the machine language subroutine. At E$+2 the hex code A2 was used. This is the operation code for the instruction, "Load the X register with the value that follows it." In our subroutine, we are loading the X register with zero. Therefore the instruction at E$+2 and the data (0) at E$+3 go together.

At E$+4, the hex code 8A was used. This is the operation code for the instruction, "Transfer the value that is in the X register to the accumulator." We are going to store this value into memory, but to do this we must first place it into the accumulator. The accumulator is quite often used as a temporary storage location in passing data from one place in the computer to another.

At E$+5, the hex code 9D is used. This is the operation code for the instruction, "Store the value that is in the accumulator into memory." This is a different mode of the store accumulator instruction. This mode adds together the memory location following the instruction to the value contained in the X register. The value in the accumulator is stored into this calculated address. The X register is used to *index* the memory location. The same instruction can be used several times to store values in different memory locations by changing the value in the X register.

At E$+8, the hex code E8 is used. This is the operation code for the instruction, "Increment the value that is in the X register." The value is increased (incremented) by one. Thus, each time the computer passes through the loop, a new memory location will be used in the instruction at E$+5.

AT E$+9, the hex code E0 is used. This is the operation code for the instruction, "Compare the value that is in the X register to the value that follows the E0 operation code." The value 0A (10 decimal) follows this instruction. Thus the value in the X register is compared with 0A (hex). This supplies the computer with a condition (X=0A or X≠0A) so that it can make a branching decision at the next instruction.

At E$+11, the hex code D0 is used. This is the Operation Code for the instruction, "Branch if the previous condition is not equal." Otherwise go on to the next sequential instruction. For values of X less than 0A, the computer will branch back to the instruction at location E$+4. When X reaches 0A, the computer will go on to the instruction at E$+13. The computer goes through this loop 10 times (for X values of 0 through 9) and then returns to the main program. The value F7 used at location E$+12 is a *signed* hexadecimal equivalent of the decimal value –9. In other words, the computer must branch *back* nine steps if the given condition is true (X≠0A). The size and direction of branches will be discussed in Chapter 5.

We'll trace through the machine language subroutine step by step later in this chapter, but let's first take a look at the BASIC program which loads, calls, and prints out the results of the machine language subroutine.

BASIC PROGRAM

```
100    REM INITIALIZE MEMORY
110    CLR:DIM E$(1), E(13)

120    REM ENTER MACHINE CODES
130    FOR N = 1 TO 13
140        READ C                    ← Read codes from DATA
150        POKE ADR(E$)+N,C          ← Place in subroutine
160    NEXT N

170    REM CALL SUBROUTINE
180    X=USR(ADR(E$)+1)

190    REM PRINT RESULTS
200    GR.0                          ← Clear screen
210    FOR N = 0 TO 9
220        PRINT PEEK(6144+N)        ← Print the counts used
230    NEXT N                           for machine language loop
240    END

250    REM DECIMAL DATA
260    DATA 104, 162, 0, 138, 157, 0, 24, 232, 22
4, 10, 208, 247, 96
```
Machine codes in decimal form
(from Figure 3-4)

The FOR-NEXT loop at lines 130 through 160 READs in the decimal equivalents of the hex codes and POKEs them into the correct memory locations for the machine language subroutine. Remember, that even though BASIC needs the data in decimal form, the codes will be inserted into memory in binary form. The first few bytes of the program will actually be stored like this:

E$+1 | 0 1 1 0 1 0 0 0 | = 64+32+8 = 104 decimal

        6   8   ← hex code

E$+2 | 1 0 1 0 0 0 1 0 | = 128+32+2 = 162 decimal

        A   2   ← hex code

E$+3 | 0 0 0 0 0 0 0 0 | = 0 decimal

        0   0   ← hex code

TRACING THROUGH THE SUBROUTINE

The best way to understand a program is to put yourself in the place of the computer and perform each instruction as it occurs in the program. Let's now trace through the operations performed by the computer in our subroutine. To do this, we will have to keep track of what is happening in register X, the accumulator, and in the memory storage locations. We might also show what is contained on the stack.

As the machine language subroutine is called, the stack contains:

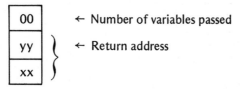

When the first machine language program is executed, the stack changes.

Address   Instruction
E$+1   Pull byte off stack

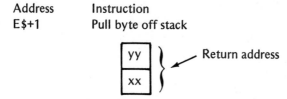

Only the return address remains. Now, the rest of the subroutine.

Address	Instruction	X	Accumulator	Memory
E$+2	Load X			
E$+3	with zero	0	—	
E$+4	Transfer X to A	0	0	
E$+5	Store accumulator			
E$+6	in (1800+X)			
E$+7		0	0	1800→ 0
E$+8	Increment X	1	0	
E$+9	Compare X			
E$+10	with 0A			
	(X = 1, not 0A)			
E$+11	Branch back to	1	0	
E$+12	E$+4 if X ≠ 0A			
E$+4	Transfer X to A	1	1	

Address	Instruction	X	Accumulator	Memory
E$+5 E$+6 E$+7	Store Accumulator in (1800+X)	1	1	1801 → ☐ 1
E$+8	Increment X	2	1	
E$+9 E$+10	Compare X with 0A	2	1	
	(X=2, not 0A)			
E$+11 E$+12	Branch back to E$+4 if X≠0A)	2	1	
E$+4	Transfer X to A	2	2	
E$+5 E$+6 E$+7	Store Accumulator in (1800+X)	2	2	1802 → ☐ 2
E$+8	Increment X	3	2	
E$+9 E$+10	Compare X with 0A	3	2	
	(X=3, not 0A)			
E$+11 E$+12	Branch back to E$+4 if X≠0A	3	2	
E$+4	Transfer X to A	3	3	
E$+5 E$+6 E$+7	Store Accumulator in (1800+X)	3	3	1803 → ☐ 3

.
.
.

This process continues with the value in X being increased by one. That value is transferred to the accumulator and then put into the memory location whose address is 1800+X.

The X register is used as a counter for the loop and also to index the memory storage (store into successive memory locations from 1800 upwards). We continue the trace after X has been incremented to 9 and the branch has been taken back to E$+4.

Address	Instruction	X	Accumulator	Memory
E$+4	Transfer X to A	9	9	
E$+5	Store Accumulator	9	9	1800 → 9
E$+6	in (1800+X)			
E$+7				
E$+8	Increment X	A	9	
E$+9	Compare X	A	9	
E$+10	with 0A			
	(X=0A, at last)			
E$+11	Branch back to	A	9	
E$+12	to E$+4 if X ≠ 0A			
E$+13	Return from Subroutine			

The return address is taken from the stack. The stack is now empty.

Thus, when the subroutine is completed, the values assigned to the X register (0 through 9) have been stored into memory.

DATA STORED BY SUBROUTINE

Hex Address	Decimal Address	Value Stored
1800	6144	0
1801	6145	1
1802	6146	2
1803	6147	3
1804	6148	4
1805	6149	5
1806	6150	6
1807	6151	7
1808	6152	8
1809	6153	9

Notice that the last value placed in the X register (0A) was not saved in memory.

When the subroutine returns to the BASIC program the values stored in the above memory locations are printed out on the screen.

```
0
1
2
3
4
5
6
7
8
9

READY
■
```

SUMMARY

In this chapter, you have learned:

- How to convert a hexadecimal number to its decimal equivalent;
- How memory is allocated in the Atari computer;
- How to set aside memory locations for a machine language subroutine;
- How to use the X index register to count the number of times that a loop is executed in a machine language program;
- How to test the X register to determine when to exit a loop;
- How to trace a machine language program by performing the instructions yourself;
- That some instructions can be used in more than one way (more than one mode);
- That the USR function can pass values from your BASIC program to your machine language program;

      1080 A=5: B=6
      1090 X=USR(ADR(E$)+1,A,B)

- That numbers passed by the USR function are pushed onto the stack as two-byte numbers;
- The following new machine language instructions:

A2	LDX	Load the X register with the value that follows.
8A	TXA	Transfer the value in the X register to the accumulator.

9D   STA   Store the accumulator's contents into the memory location that follows, *indexed* by the X register.

E8   INX   Increment the value in the X register.

E0   CPX   Compare the value in the X register to the value that follows.

D0   BNE   Branch forward, or back, the number of steps given if condition is not equal to zero.

EXERCISES

1. Convert the following hexadecimal numbers to their decimal equivalents.

        A2 hex = _____ decimal

        3B hex = _____ decimal

        9E hex = _____ decimal

```
+-------------------------------------------------+
|                                                 |
|                                                 |
|                                                 |
|                  work space                     |
|                                                 |
|                                                 |
|                                                 |
+-------------------------------------------------+
```

2. It is not safe (or at least caution must be used) to POKE _____
    BASIC, machine
    language instructions in the area of memory below your _____
    BASIC, machine
    language program instructions.

3. If your BASIC program dimensions the string variable E$ to one, you are saving space in the memory area above your BASIC program. At what address would it be safe to start a machine language program called from your BASIC program? _____

4. Does the location saved for E$ depend upon the length of your BASIC program? _____

5. Data assigned to variables can be passed from a BASIC program to a machine language subroutine. Even though no variables are passed to the sub-

routine, the subroutine must perform some operation on the stack *before* a
return can be made from the subroutine. What is that operation?

_____

_____

6. Suppose that the X register contains the value 7, and the accumulator holds
   the value 1A. The computer executes the instruction:

       E$+7   9D   STA 1800, X
       E$+8   00
       E$+9   18

   In what memory location is the value 1A stored?

   _____

7. The BASIC program of page 44 and the subroutine of page 42 are to be
   executed. The only change made is to line 210 of the BASIC program. It is
   changed to:

       210 FOR N = 3 TO 5

   Show what will be printed on the screen when the program is executed.

   ← Answer here

8. What changes would be made to the machine language subroutine on page
   42 if you wanted the loop to count to 20 decimal instead of 10 decimal?

       _____   _____

       address   hex code

9. What changes would you make to the BASIC program on page 44 to print
   out the 20 values stored by the changed machine language program (exercise 8)?

   _____

       260 DATA _____

   _____

ANSWERS

1. A2 hex = 162 decimal
   3B hex = 59 decimal
   9E hex = 158 decimal

2. Machine
   BASIC

3. E$+1 or ADR(E$)+1

4. Yes (Space is saved for E$ at the end of your BASIC program.)

5. One byte must be pulled off the top of the stack (the number that tells how many variables were passed, zero in this case) before the return address is available.

6. Location 1807 (1800+7) ─────────── the value in X

7.

3
4
5

READY
■

8. E$+10   14   (16+4 = 20)

9. Line 210 FOR N = 0 TO 19
Line 260 DATA 104,162,0,138,157,0,24,232,22,
4,20,208,247,95

change these values

Chapter 4

Getting Started
With the Assembler

Only the 400 or 800 computer and the Assembler Cartridge are necessary to write, assemble, and execute assembly language programs. However, some storage device (an Atari 410 Program Recorder or Atari 810 Disk Drive) is recommended. Otherwise, you will have to enter your program from the keyboard each time that you want to use it. The Atari 820 printer is an optional addition. It will allow you to make permanent records of your programs in a form that is easy to read.

In writing this book, the authors used the system elements shown below in solid lines. Those elements in broken lines are optional.

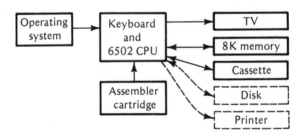

Figure 4-1. Our Atari 800 System

Communication between elements of the Atari 400/800 system is managed by the Atari Operating System contained in a 10K ROM (10,000-byte Read Only Memory) using some associated RAM (Random Access Memory). The Assembler taps into the Operating System as needed.

The Atari Assembler Cartridge contains three separate programs:

1. The **Writer/Editor**
2. The **Assembler**
3. The **Debugger**

The **Writer/Editor Program**, just as the name implies, is used to write and edit your assembly language programs. Assembly language is a shorthand that uses English like abbreviations to represent instructions to the computer. It also uses numbers in decimal or hexadecimal form to provide data for the programs.

The **Assembler Program** translates the abbreviations provided by the **Writer/ Editor** into machine language codes and data that the computer can understand. It also takes care of assigning the instructions and data to their proper memory locations.

The **Debugger Program** is used to execute, test, or trace the operation of the machine language program that the **Assembler** produced.

You can see that the three programs are used in a logical order. If the **De-bugger** produces a faulty program, you may return to the **Writer/Editor Program** for changes. The process is then repeated until satisfactory results are obtained. Here is a diagram of the order in which the three programs are used.

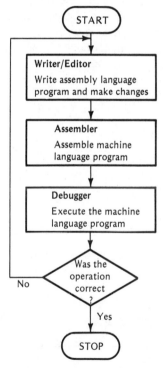

Figure 4-2. Use Flow of Assembler Cartridge

THE WRITER/EDITOR

Before we get too involved in the technicalities of assembly and machine language, let's power up the computer and try a short sample program.

Place the Assembler Cartridge in the left slot of the computer, make sure that your TV set is connected and turned on, and turn on the computer. This is what you should see on the screen:

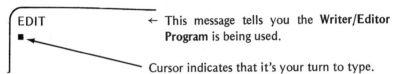

EDIT   ← This message tells you the **Writer/Editor Program** is being used.

Cursor indicates that it's your turn to type.

A small amount of memory space (108 locations) is used to store the characters typed in for the line that you are currently typing. This area or memory is called the *Current Line Buffer*. The buffer is written over as each new line is typed in. It is located in an area of 384 locations (180 HEX) which is reserved for the Assembler Cartridge.

An area of memory just above that saved for the Assembler is used for the Edit Text Buffer. It stores all the input from the keyboard as you are writing the Assembly Language Program. As you enter more and more from the keyboard, the Edit Text Buffer fills up. No upper bound is specified. However, it is possible to exceed the memory limits of your computer.

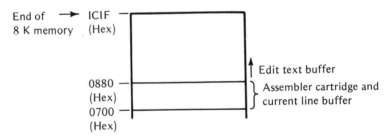

Figure 4-3. Buffer Memory

To find the location of the Current Line Buffer and the Edit Text Buffer, type the command:

SIZE (and press the RETURN key)

The display:

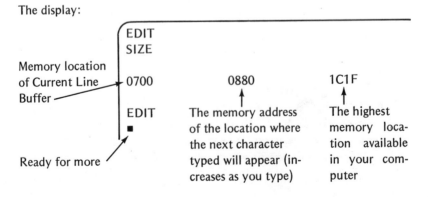

The numbers displayed will differ according to the amount of memory in your system. Remember, our system is the Atari 800 with 8K or RAM and no disk.

You can find out, at any time, how long your program is by using the SIZE command. Subtract the first number (700 in our case) + 180 from the second number. The result is the approximate number of characters in your program.

Before we enter our program, let's take a look at the format used for writing assembly language programs. The program to be assembled is called a **Source Program**. The **Source Program** consists of statements just as a BASIC program does. The statements are numbered just as BASIC lines are numbered. Every statement must start with a line number in the range of 0 through 65535. After each statement is entered using the **Writer/Editor Program** of the Assembler Cartridge, it is terminated (or entered) by pressing the RETURN key.

The format used for each statement is divided into five fields.

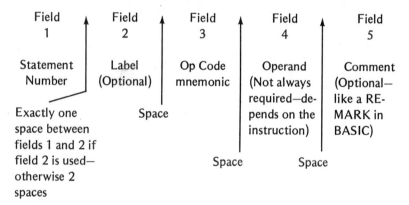

Field 1	Field 2	Field 3	Field 4	Field 5
Statement Number	Label (Optional)	Op Code mnemonic	Operand (Not always required—depends on the instruction)	Comment (Optional—like a REMARK in BASIC)

Exactly one space between fields 1 and 2 if field 2 is used—otherwise 2 spaces

Space

Space   Space

Examples:

1. No label used

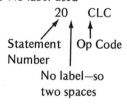

```
      20  CLC
```
Statement Number | Op Code

No label—so two spaces

This instruction—Clear the Carry bit

2. No label used

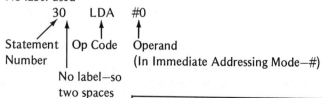

```
      30  LDA  #0
```
Statement Number | Op Code | Operand (In Immediate Addressing Mode—#)

No label—so two spaces

This instruction—Put zero in the accumulator

3. Label used

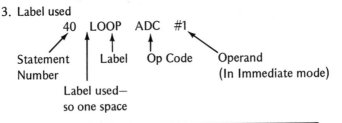

This instruction—Add one to the value in accumulator

4. No label used

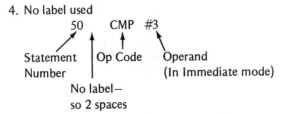

This instruction—Compare the value in accumulator with 3

5. No label—operand gives branch location

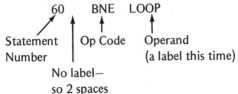

This instruction—If the 2 values are *not* equal, go back to the instruction
with the LOOP label

Now, let's write an assembly language program using the above statements. When we left the computer, it was in the Edit mode.

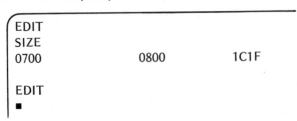

```
EDIT
SIZE
0700            0800            1C1F

EDIT
■
```

We must first tell the assembler where to start our machine language program, called the **Object Program**, in memory. We do this with a special command.

The starting memory location of the machine language program must be high enough above the Edit Text Buffer (0880 in our case) so that the two programs do not overlap.

Type: 10   *=$1000

Line   2 spaces   Starting address ($ indicates a hexadecimal value)
number

Then the balance of the program is entered. Remember to press the RETURN key at the end of each line (just like you do in BASIC).

```
20      CLC
30      LDA #0
40      LOOP ADC #1
50      CMP #3
60      BNE LOOP
```

The program must conclude with an END statement (called a PSEUDO OPERA-TOR or _Directive_). Every program should have one and only one END Directive.

```
70      END
```

one space

THE ASSEMBLER PROGRAM

After the program has been entered using the **Writer/Editor Program**, the next step is performed by the **Assembler Program**. The assembler will convert the assembly language instructions to machine language codes and assign memory locations to the machine language codes.

The video screen at this time (before going to the **Assembler Program**) shows:

```
EDIT
10    *=$1000
20    CLC
30    LDA #0
40    LOOP ADC #1
50    CMP #3
60    BNE LOOP
70    END
```

Let's check to see how much memory has been used by our assembly language program. Remember, when we typed SIZE earlier, we saw:

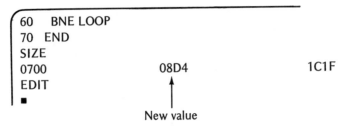

To see how much memory has been used, once again type: SIZE.

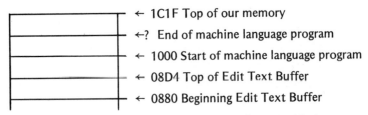

New value

Our program has used 8D4-880 or 54 (hex) memory locations:

	← 1C1F Top of our memory
	←? End of machine language program
	← 1000 Start of machine language program
	← 08D4 Top of Edit Text Buffer
	← 0880 Beginning Edit Text Buffer

Notice that there is an unused area between the assembly language program (Edit Text Buffer) and the machine language program. That is good. When longer assembly language programs are used, care must be taken that machine language and assembly language programs do not overlap. We can now proceed to the **Assembler Program.**

You now type: ASM (and press the RETURN key)

Each machine code is displayed followed by the assembly language instructions that created it.

```
     .
     .
     .
60    END
ASM
0000            10            *=    $1000

1000  18         20           CLC

1001  A900       30           LDA #0

1003  6901      40 LOOP       ADC #1
```

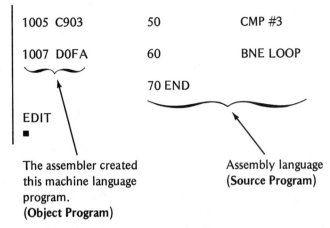

| 1005 C903 | 50 | CMP #3 |
| 1007 D0FA | 60 | BNE LOOP |

70 END

EDIT
■

The assembler created
this machine language
program.
(Object Program)

Assembly language
(Source Program)

The assembly language **Source Program** that you entered is shown on the right side of the screen. The machine language **Object Program** that the assembler produced is shown on the left side of the screen with the memory locations that were assigned to each machine language instruction. Let's examine the programs line by line to see how the instructions match up.

Machine Language	Assembly Language
ASM 0000	10 *= $1000 Line 10 assigned the starting address of the machine language program to 1000 (hex).
1000 18	20 CLC The instruction CLC is assembled into the machine language code: 18. The instruction 18 is placed in memory location 1000.
1001 A900	30 LDA #0 The instruction LDA #0 is assembled into the machine language code: A900. The instruction A9 (from LDA #) is placed in memory location 1001, and the data (00) is placed in location 1002.
1003 6901	40 LOOP ADC #1 The instruction ADC #1 is assembled into the machine language code: 6901. The instruction 69 (from ADC #) is placed in memory location 1003, and the data (01) in location 1004.

1005 C903	50	CMP #3

The instruction CMP #3 is assembled into the machine language code: C903. The instruction C9 (from CMP #) is placed in memory location 1005, and the data (03) in location 1006.

1007 D0FA	60	BNE LOOP

The instruction BNE LOOP is assembled into the machine language code: D0FA. The instruction D0 (from BNE) is placed in location 1007, and the length of the branch (FA) is placed in location 1008. The branch if taken goes back to memory location 1003 where the LOOP began.

70 END

Line 70 tells the assembler where to stop. No machine code is created.

We have used five assembly language instructions in this program. These instructions consist of a *mnemonic* code that is an abbreviation of its English language meaning and usually an operand. These meanings are given below.

Mnemonic	Operand		Meaning
CLC			CLear the Carry bit of the Processor Status Register (set it to zero).

| LDA | #0 | = | LoaD Accumulator with the immediate operand (#0) |

| ADC | #1 | = | ADd to accumulator with Carry the immediate operand (#1). |

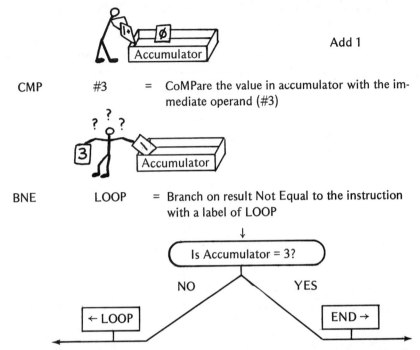

Add 1

CMP   #3   =   CoMPare the value in accumulator with the immediate operand (#3)

BNE   LOOP   =   Branch on result Not Equal to the instruction with a label of LOOP

The machine language program has been assembled and is stored in the computer's memory as follows:

Memory Location	Machine Code	
1000	18	Instruction CLC
1001	A9	Instruction LDA #
1002	00	Data loaded
1003	69	Instruction ADC #
1004	01	Data to be added
1005	C9	Instruction CMP #
1006	03	Data to be compared
1007	D0	Instruction BNE
1008	FA	Data telling where to branch

Figure 4-4. Machine Language Program Storage

EXECUTING THE MACHINE LANGUAGE PROGRAM—
THE DEBUGGER

You have used the **Writer/Editor Program** to write the assembly language program and the **Assembler Program** to assemble it into machine language codes and allocate memory locations. It's now time to use the **Debugger Program** to execute (or run) the machine language program.

After the program was assembled, you probably noticed that the computer returned to the **Writer/Editor Program** and displayed the word EDIT followed on the next line by the cursor.

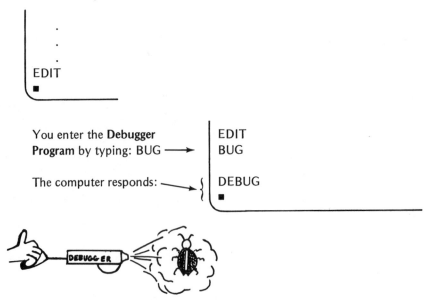

You enter the **Debugger Program** by typing: BUG ──────▶

The computer responds: ──────▶

```
EDIT
BUG

DEBUG
■
```

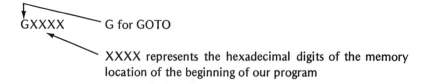

The computer is now waiting for a DEBUGGER command. There are several, but we'll only look at two of them right now to avoid confusion. The first has the form:

GXXXX ── G for GOTO

XXXX represents the hexadecimal digits of the memory location of the beginning of our program

If you type: G1000 (and press the RETURN key), the program will execute immediately. You will see the following on the display:

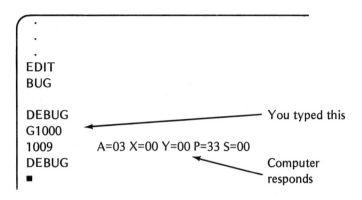

What does all this mean?

1. The number 1009 tells you that the program stopped at this memory location. It executed all the instructions from location 1000 *through* 1008.

2. The only other value on the line that we are presently concerned with is: A=03. A stands for Accumulator. The value 03 shows that the accumulator holds a value of 3 when the program ended. This is just what we wanted. Our program put an original value of 0 in the accumulator (LDA #0). It then added a 1 each time through the loop until the accumulator contained a value of 3. Then the computer stopped.

Let's watch it count, step by step, as the program is executed. Notice that the DEBUG message was displayed at the end of the previous program execution. This means that we are still in the **Debugger Program** and can try out our second DEBUGGER command. We can perform a step-by-step *trace* of the program by typing:

T for TRACE   Starting memory location 1000

This is what we then see on the display:

```
1000        18       CLC            } ← { The top two lines will }
   A=00 X=00 Y=00 P=32 S=00              scroll off the screen

1001        A9 00    LDA     #$00
   A=00 X=00 Y=00 P=32 S=00
1003        69 01    ADC     #$01   ← One added to accumulator
   A=01 X=00 Y=00 P=30 S=00
1005        C9 03    CMP     #$03
   A=01 X=00 Y=00 P=B0 S=00
1007        D0 FA    BNE     $1003
   A=01 X=00 Y=00 P=B0 S=00
1003        69 01    ADC     #$01   ← Branch back and add 1 more
   A=02 X=00 Y=00 P=30 S=00
1005        C9 03    CMP     #$03
   A=02 X=00 Y=00 P=B0 S=00
1007        D0 FA    BNE     $1003
   A=02 X=00 Y=00 P=B0 S=00
1003        69 01    ADC     #$01   ← Branch back and add 1 more
   A=03 X=00 Y=00 P=30 S=00
1005        C9 03    CMP     #$03
   A=03 X=00 Y=00 P=33 S=00           Now comparison is equal—
1007        D0 FA    BNE     $1003    so no branch
   A=03 X=00 Y=00 P=33 S=00
1009        00       BRK              BRK for break—program
   A=03 X=00 Y=00 P=33 S=00           stops
DEBUG
■
```

Figure 4-5. Program Trace

Notice that the Accumulator (A) increases by one each time the ADC #01 instruction is executed at location 1003. The value in the accumulator is shown following each instruction line as: A=nn (where nn is a two-digit hex value). The values that you see in the other registers may differ from that shown here. Do not worry about them for the time being. You should only be concerned with the accumulator at this time. Registers are covered in Chapter 5.

If you want to see how fast the computer can count to 255 (FF HEX), let's modify the compare value at line 50 to:

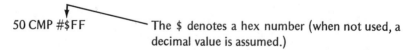

50 CMP #$FF   The $ denotes a hex number (when not used, a decimal value is assumed.)

With this modification, the computer will not stop when the value in the accumulator equals 3 but will go right on to FF. We could enter a whole new program to accomplish this change, but it's easier to alter the program that we already have.

We left the computer in the **Debugger Program** after tracing our last program. We need to get back to the **Writer/Editor Program** to change line 50.

Type : X (and press RETURN)

```
      .
      .
      .
1009        00              BRK
  A = 03 X = 00 Y=00 P=33 S=00
DEBUG                              ←    You type the X
X

EDIT
■
```

To take a look at the previous **Assembler Program**, guess what command is used.

Type: LIST (and press RETURN)

Just like
-BASIC

```
   .
   .
   .
EDIT
LIST

10     *=$1000
20     CLC
30     LDA #0
40     LOOP ADC #1
50     CMP #3
60     BNE LOOP
70     END
■
```

All that you have to do to change line 50 is to type in the new line (with the line number of course).

Type: 50   CMP   #$FF   (Don't forget the $ sign.)

```
        .
        .
        .
70    END
50      CMP #$FF
■
```

To verify that the change has been made, LIST the program again.

```
        .
        .
        .
70    END
50      CMP #$FF
LIST

10      *=$1000
20      CLC
30      LDA #0
40      LOOP ADC #1
50      CMP #$FF          ←   Yes, the change was made.
60      BNE LOOP
70      END
```

Another way to replace the value to be compared would be by the Editor's REPLACE statement. We could have accessed the Edit mode and typed:

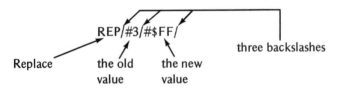

REP/#3/#$FF/   three backslashes

Replace   the old   the new
               value   value

The result would have been the same.

Even though the change has been made to the assembly language program, it has _not_ been made to the machine language program. We must _assemble_ the modified program.

Type: ASM   (and press RETURN)

```
      .
      .
      .
60      END
ASM
0000            10        *=      $1000
1000  18        20        CLC
1001  A900      30        LDA  #0
1003  6901      40 LOOP   ADC #1
1005  C9FF      50        CMP  #$FF
1007  D0FA      60        BNE  LOOP
                70  END

EDIT
▪
```

Remember, we must use the **Debugger Program** to execute the program. So type: BUG

```
      .
      .
      .
EDIT
BUG

DEBUG
▪
```

Now run the program by typing: G1000

```
DEBUG
G1000
1009            A=FF X=00 Y=00 P=33 S=00
DEBUG                    There it is
▪
```

Wow, that was quick! How do we know the computer didn't just print the final result instead of counting all the way? Let's slow it down by tracing the program.

Keep your eye on the column that prints the value in the accumulator (A). The results will go by pretty fast as the screen fills up and *scrolls* upward. It will take between 2 and 3 minutes for the accumulator to reach FF.

Type: T1000   (and press RETURN)

The screen scrolls merrily on its way. After some time it finally stops at the end of the program.

```
.
.
.
1007              D0 FA            BNE $1003
        A=FF X=00 Y=00 P=33 S=00
1009               00              BRK
        A=FF X=00 Y=00 P=33 S=00
DEBUG
■
```

Yes, it really did count up to FF.

It did take awhile for the computer to trace through the program. That's because it had to look up and print out all those values in the registers. It works much faster when you leave it alone and don't ask it to perform any extra tasks.

We have found out that we can increase the value in the accumulator by adding one to it. We can also subtract values from the accumulator. Why not start with a value of FF and subtract one from it each time through the loop? To do this we need two new instructions.

SBC   (SuBtract from accumulator with borrow; borrow is the opposite of Carry, but they call it SBC)

SEC   (set the Carry bit. This will replace the Clear Carry instruction.)

We can use our old program to model the new one.

ADD PROGRAM					SUBTRACT PROGRAM	
10	*=$1000				10	*=$1000
20	CLC	←	Clear and set	→	20	SEC
30	LDA #0	←	Start at	→	30	LDA #$FF
40	LOOP ADC #1	← Add and Subtract →			40	LOOP SBC #1
50	CMP #$FF	←	Go until	→	50	CMP #0
60	BNE LOOP				60	BNE LOOP
70	END				70	END

If you still have the **Add Program** in memory (check by entering the **Writer/ Editor Program** and LISTing the program), you can change lines 20, 30, 40, and 50. Then assemble the new program. Otherwise, enter the complete new **Subtract Program**, and then assemble it.

After assembling the new program, enter the **Debugger Program** and execute it by typing:

G1000

```
EDIT
BUG

DEBUG
G1000
1009              A=00 X=00 Y=00 P=33 S=00
DEBUG            ↑
■                It quickly counts down to zero.
```

You can verify the action by using the trace feature. Use the BREAK key to stop the program at a convenient point. As shown by the following display, we stopped ours shortly after it started.

Type: T1000

```
DEBUG
T1000
1000              38              SEC
     A=00 X=00 Y=00 P=B1 S=00
1001              A9 FF           LDA #$FF
     A=FF X=00 Y=00 P=B1 S=00
1003              E9 01           SBC #$01
     A=FE X=00 Y=00 P=B1 S=00
1005              C9 00           CMP #$00
     A=FE X=00 Y=00 P=B1 S=00
1007              D0 FA           BNE $100
     A=FE X=00 Y=00 P=B1 S=00
1003              E9 01           SBC #$01
     A=FD X=00 Y=00 P=B1 S=00
1005              C9 00           CMP #$00
     A=FD X=00 Y=00 P=B1 S=00
1007       ↑      D               ←  We pressed the BREAK key
DEBUG      |                         here.
■          |
     Accumulator down from FF to FD
```

If you let the program execute until the accumulator counts down to zero, you'll find out that the computer can count backwards just as fast as forwards. Keep your eye on the Accumulator as the data scrolls by.

Let's take a break now to sum up what you have learned so far. Several small doses of assembly language are easier to take than a few very large ones. A more complete coverage of the Assembler features is summarized in Chapter 7.

SUMMARY

The Assembler Cartridge consists of 3 programs:

1. **Writer/Editor**—Used to write and edit assembly language programs.

2. **Assembler**—Used to translate assembly instructions into machine code and to assign memory locations for the machine language program.

3. **Debugger**—Used to execute machine language programs.

Key Words Used
Writer/Editor

1. EDIT—a prompt to let you know you are in the **Writer/Editor Program**.

2. SIZE—Displays memory locations of Current Line Buffer, Edit Text Buffer, and your machine's highest available memory.

3. LIST—Lists the assembly language program on the video screen.

4. BUG—A command that transfers control from the **Writer/Editor Program** to the **Debugger Program**.

5. ASM—A command that transfers control from the **Writer/Editor Program** to the **Assembler Program**.

Debugger

1. DEBUG—A prompt to let you know that you are in the **Debugger Program**.

2. GXXXX—A command which executes the current machine language program beginning at memory location XXXX (each X is a hex digit).

3. TXXXX—A command to trace each step of the current machine language program as it is executing from memory location XXXX (each X is again a hex digit).

4. X—A command that transfers control from the **Debugger Program** to the **Writer/Editor Program**.

Instructions Used:

Assembly Language Instructions (for Source Program)	Machine Language Code Produced (for Object Program)	Comments
LDA#0	A9 00	Load accumulator with zero—Immediate Addressing mode
ADC #1	69 01	Add 1 to the accumulator—Immediate Addressing mode
CMP #3	C9 03	Compare value in accumulator with 3—Immediate Addressing mode

BNE LOOP	D0 FA	Branch on result not equal to zero back to the instruction labeled LOOP—Relative Addressing mode
END		A Directive—no machine code is generated.
SBC #1	E9 01	Subtract 1 from the value in the accumulator—Immediate Addressing mode.
CLC	18	Clear the Carry bit
SEC	38	Set the Carry bit to 1

EXERCISES

1. Assembly language programs are written using the _____ Program of the Assembler Cartridge.
2. The _____ Program of the Assembler Cartridge is used to translate assembler language programs to machine code.
3. Machine language programs are executed from the _____ Program of the Assembler Cartridge.
4. The **Source Program** is assembled into the _____ Program.
5. The function of LDA #0 is to load the accumulator with zero. Give the function of the following assembly language instructions.
   (a) LDA #$FF _____
   (b) ADC #10 _____
   (c) CMP #$1E _____

Exercises 6 through 10 refer to this assembled program.

```
ASM
0000              10      *=  $1000
1000   18         20      CLC
1001   A9 01      30      LDA #1
1003   69 02      40 LOOP ADC #2
1005   C9 03      50      CMP #9
1007   D0 FA      60      BNE LOOP
                  70 END
```

Machine language   Assembly language
   program   program

6. The accumulator is first loaded with what number? _____

7. What number is added each time through the loop? _____

8. What will be the number in the accumulator when the program has passed through the loop the last time? _____

9. If a trace of the machine language program was executed, the trace would display accumulator values that are _____ from _____
(odd, even)

through _____ .

10. Lines 30 and 50 in the assembly language program could be changed so that the display of a trace would display accumulator values that were even from 0 through 8. Show the two modified assembly language lines that would make this change.

30 _____

50 _____

ANSWERS

1. Writer/Editor
2. Assembler
3. Debugger
4. Object
5. (a) Load the accumulator with FF (hex)
   (b) Add 10 to the accumulator (10 is decimal—no $ sign)
   (c) Compare the value in the accumulator with 1E (hex)
6. 1
7. 2
8. 9
9. odd, 1, 9
10. 30   LDA #0
    50   CMP #8

Chapter 5

Special-Purpose Registers and Addressing Modes

The 6502 microprocessor used in the Atari 400/800 computers has several special-purpose registers. These registers hold 8 bits (1 byte) of data just like memory locations but are used for special purposes. You have seen displays of the data contained in these registers in the trace of the program in Chapter 4.

Example:

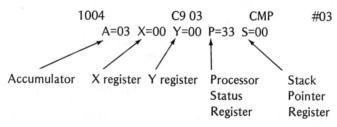

```
        1004          C9 03        CMP      #03
              A=03  X=00  Y=00  P=33  S=00
```

Accumulator   X register Y register Processor   Stack
                                       Status   Pointer
                                       Register   Register

We will discuss these special registers in the order listed below.

1. The Accumulator—Most operations on data are performed here. You can tell from the short program in Chapter 4 that the accumulator is a very busy place.

2. The X register—This register is used as a scratch pad or as an index in certain addressing modes.

3. The Y register—This register is used in the same way as the X register.

4. The Processor Status Register—This register contains a record of the microprocessor's status as each instruction is executed. Each bit of this register holds one item of status information.

5. The Stack Pointer Register—The data in this register is the memory location of the top of the stack. The stack is a special block of memory at addresses 01FF down through 0100 (hex).

THE ACCUMULATOR

The programs in Chapters 3 and 4 showed how the accumulator can be loaded with a number in the Immediate Addressing mode. One program also added a number to this value (using the Immediate Addressing mode) and then compared the result with the value 3 (again in the Immediate Addressing mode). All of those operations were performed using only the accumulator and data held in certain memory locations of the program.

A branch instruction (BNE in the Relative Addressing mode) was also used in the program. To determine whether to take the branch or not, the computer examined the Processor Status Register. It looked at one bit (the zero bit) of the Processor Status register.

THE X AND Y REGISTERS

Let's now develop a short program to demonstrate some action taking place in the X register. It will be very similar to the programs used in Chapters 3 and 4.

1. LDX #0   Load the X register (LDX) with zero using the Immediate Addressing mode (#0).

2. INX   Increment the X register (INX) using the Implied Addressing mode (no operand used).

3. CPX #3   Compare the value in the X register (CPX) with 3 using the Immediate Addressing mode (#3).

4. BNE LOOP   Branch if the result (X register–3) is *not* equal to zero (BNE) back to the instruction that you have *labeled* LOOP (INX in this program).

The program is written using the **Writer/Editor Program** of the Assembler cartridge as before. When you are in the Edit mode, type NEW to erase any old program that may still be in the Edit Buffer. This does not erase the memory contents (the previously assembled machine language program). Enter the program as shown.

```
EDIT
10    *=$1000
20    LDX #0
30 LOOP INX          ← You enter this.
40    CPX #3
50    BNE LOOP
60 END
■
```

Then you use the **Assembler Program** to assemble the machine language program.

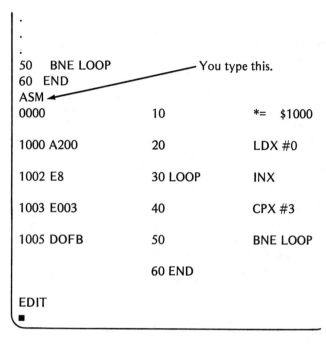

Now enter the **Debugger Program** and execute the run.

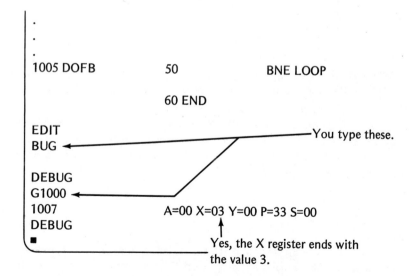

This time, trace the program step by step. Type: T1000

WATCH
the
X reg.
go up
at
1002

```
1000      A2    00            LDX  #$00
          A=00 X=00 Y=00 P=32 S=00
1002      E8                  INX
          A=00 X=01 Y=00 P=30 S=00
1003      E0    03            CPX  #$03
          A=00 X=01 Y=00 P=B0 S=00
1005      D0    FB            BNE  $1002    ← The
          A=00 X=01 Y=00 P=B0 S=00                assembler
1002      E8                  INX                 calculated
          A=00 X=02 Y=00 P=30 S=00                this branch
1003      E0    03            CPX  #$03            location.
          A=00 X=02 Y=00 P=B0 S=00
1005      D0    FB            BNE  $1002    Your X
          A=00 X=02 Y=00 P=B0 S=00             register
1002      E8                  INX              should be
          A=00 X=03 Y=00 P=30 S=00             displayed
1003      E0    03            CPX  #$03         as ours is.
          A=00 X=03 Y=00 P=33 S=00             The other
1005      D0    FB            BNE  $1002     registers
          A=00 X=03 Y=00 P=33 S=00             may
1007      00                  BRK              differ.
          A=00 X=03 Y=00 P=33 S=00
DEBUG
■
```

Notice that the value in the X register increases each time that the computer executes INX at location 1002. Notice also that the program stops at location 1007 with the instruction BRK (BREAK).

The computer uses the BREAK instruction to stop itself at the end of a program. We'll discuss the BRK instruction more thoroughly in Chapter 9.

Next, let's modify the program to count in both the accumulator and the X register. We'll use one new instruction:

TAX

No, it's not really tax time. This is just a mnemonic code that stands for: Transfer Accumulator to X register. When this instruction is executed, the data currently in the accumulator is transferred to (or copied into) the X register. The data also stays in the accumulator.

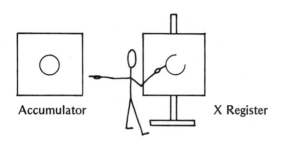

Accumulator   X Register

Copy accumulator into X register (TAX)

Type: X and press the RETURN key to get back to the Writer/Editor mode. Now you can erase the old program by typing:

NEW

Wow! This is just like BASIC. The old program is erased and you are ready to write the new program.

PROGRAM TO COUNT IN ACCUMULATOR

AND IN THE X REGISTER

```
EDIT
10    *=$1000
20    CLC                         New Instruction, Transfer
30    LDA #0                      content of Accumulator to
40    TAX              ←          the X register
50  LOOP ADC #1         ←          Add 1 to accumulator
60    INX              ←          Increment X register
70    CPX #3
80    BNE LOOP
90  END
■
```

Then assemble it:

```
        .
        .
        .
80    BNE LOOP
90   END
ASM
0000                    10              *=        $1000

1000    18              20              CLC

1001    A900            30              LDA #0

1003    AA              40              TAX

1004    6901            50 LOOP         ADC #1

1006    E8              60              INX

1007    E003            70              CPX #3

1009    D0F9            80              BNE LOOP

                        90 END

EDIT
■
```

Now enter the **Debugger Program.**

```
        .
        .
        .
EDIT
BUG

DEBUG
■
```

To see what happens as a program is executed, the trace feature of the assembler is a tremendous aid. Let's use it again to watch our program in action.

Type: T1000 and press the RETURN key

```
1007    E0  03                    CPX    #$03
   A=01 X=01 Y=00 P=B0 S=00
1009    D0  F9                    BNE    $1004
   A=01 X=01 Y=00 P=B0 S=00
1004    69  01                    ADC    #$01
   A=02 X=01 Y=00 P=30 S=00
1006    E8                        INX
   A=02 X=02 Y=00 P=30 S=00
1007    E0  03                    CPX    #$03
   A=02 X=02 Y=00 P=B0 S=00
1009    D0  F9                    BNE    $1004
   A=02 X=02 Y=00 P=B0 S=00
1004    69  01                    ADC    #$01
   A=03 X=02 Y=00 P=30 S=00
1006    E8                        INX
   A=03 X=03 Y=00 P=30 S=00
1007    E0  03                    CPX    #$03
   A=03 X=03 Y=00 P=33 S=00
1009    D0  F9                    BNE    $1004
   A=03 X=03 Y=00 P=33 S=00
100B    00                        BRK
   A=03 X=03 Y=00 P=33 S=00
DEBUG
■
```

What happened? The first part of the program rolled by so fast that we couldn't read it. The video screen can only hold 24 lines of information at one time. Now what?

Looking in the Atari Assembler Manual, I see a DEBUGGER command:

SXXXX   Single-step operation

Let's try that. The instructions in the manual say to type in S followed by the address of the first instruction. Then type S and press the RETURN key. Do this last operation repeatedly to see each step. Here goes.

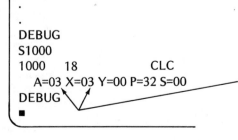

```
      .
      .
      .
DEBUG
S1000
1000    18              CLC
   A=03 X=03 Y=00 P=32 S=00
DEBUG
■
```

The value 3 is left over from the last program. NEW does not change the machine language memory *or* registers only the Text Edit Buffer.

The computer stops here, but it's only waiting for you to type an S and press RETURN. So . . .

```
.
.
.
.
.
S
1001    A9 00          LDA          #$00         Accumulator
   A=00 X=03 Y=00 P=32 S=00                      cleared to zero
DEBUG
S
1003    AA             TAX                        X register
   A=00 X=00 Y=00 P=32 S=00                      cleared to zero
DEBUG
S
1004    69 01          ADC          #$01      ←One added to
   A=01 X=00 Y=00 P=30 S=00                      accumulator
DEBUG
S
1006    E8             INX                     ← X register
   A=01 X=01 Y=00 P=30 S=00                      incremented
DEBUG
S
1007    E0 03          CPX          #$03
   A=01 X=01 Y=00 P=B0 S=00
DEBUG
S
1009    D0 F9          BNE          $1004
   A=01 X=01 Y=00 P=B0 S=00
DEBUG
S
1004    69 01          ADC          #$01      ← One added
   A=02 X=01 Y=00 P=30 S=00                      again to
DEBUG                                             accumulator
S
1006    E8             INX                     ← X register
   A=02 X=02 Y=00 P=30 S=00                      incremented
          .                                       again
          .
          .
```

```
        this continues until X=03
                    .
                    .
                    .
                    .
                    .

1007    E0 03           CPX         #$03        ← Is X=3?
   A=03 X=03 Y=00 P=33 S=00
DEBUG                                           Yes
S
1009    D0 F9           BNE         $1003       ← Do not
   A=03 X=03 Y=00 P=33 S=00                        branch this
DEBUG                                              time
S
100B    00              BRK
   A=03 X=03 Y=00 P=33 S=00
DEBUG
■
```

We have now used the A (accumulator) and the X registers. Since the Y register is used in the same way as the X register, we will pass it over for the time being. You no doubt noticed that the value in the Y register did not change in each of the programs that we used.

Before we leave this program, let's go back to the **Writer/Editor Program.** You do this by typing an X and pressing the RETURN key.

```
  .
  .
  .
DEBUG
X

EDIT
■
```

Remember, you can list assembly language programs in the assembler's **Writer/Editor Program** just like you LIST in BASIC.

```
.
.
.
EDIT
LIST

10   *=$1000
20   CLC
30   LDA #0
40   TAX
50   LOOP ADC #1
60   INX
70   CPX #3
80   BNE LOOP
90   END
■
```

This feature of the **Writer/Editor Program** can be very helpful when editing a program to make changes due to programming errors or to make modifications for any other reason.

THE PROCESSOR STATUS REGISTER

This register holds seven bits of information about the status of the microprocessor. The eighth bit of the register is not used. The individual information bits are called *flags*. These flags are always in one of two conditions: SET to one (1) or RESET to zero (0). The flags are called: Carry, Zero result, Interrupt disable, Decimal mode, Break command, Overflow, and Negative result. Here is the position that each flag occupies in the register.

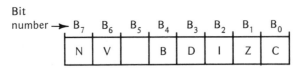

Figure 5-1. Processor Status Register

where: N = Negative result
V = Overflow
B = Break command
D = Decimal mode
I = Interrupt disable
Z = Zero result
C = Carry

B_0, Carry bit   This bit is modified as a result of certain arithmetic and logic operations. It can also be SET or RESET by programmed instruction. We will be using it later.

B_1, Zero bit   This flag is automatically SET when any data movement or arithmetic operation has a result equal to zero. It was tested by the BNE (Branch on result not equal) in the programs of Chapter 4 and Chapter 5. See page 59 for an example.

B_2, Interrupt disable bit   This flag controls the effect of the interrupt request pin of the microprocessor. We will not be concerned with this bit for now.

B_3, Decimal mode bit   This flag controls whether or not the addition and subtraction operations are performed by the computer as binary or decimal. More on this later.

B_4, Break command bit   This bit is SET only by the microprocessor. It is used during interrupts. It appeared in our display at the end of the programs when we had executed a trace or single-step execution.

B_5, Expansion bit   This bit is not used at present. It is reserved for future expansion of the 6502 microprocessor.

B_6, Overflow bit   This bit is used to indicate that an overflow has occurred in a signed binary arithmetic operation. More on this later when we get to signed number arithmetic operations.

B_7, Negative bit   This bit tells whether the result of some arithmetic operation is negative or not. We'll discuss this in detail when we get to signed number arithmetic operations.

It may seem like we are putting you off on many of the flags in the Processor Status Register. We are! We'll introduce each of the flags as they are used by our programs. The first one that you have encountered is the Zero flag.

If you look back to the trace of the program in Figure 4-5, the first and second execution of the CMP #3 instruction at location 1005 shows:

```
First
execution   →  1005  C9 03              CMP   #$03
                   A=01 X=00 Y=00 P=B0 S=00
                      .
                      .
                      .
Second          .
execution   →  1005 C9 03               CMP   #$03
                   A=02 X=00 Y=00 P=B0 S=00
                                    ⟋
```

Notice that the Processor Status Register (P) holds the value B0.

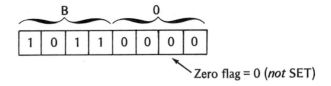

Zero flag = 0 (*not* SET)

This means that when the value in the accumulator was compared to 3, the result (1-3 or 2-3) was *not* equal to zero.

Therefore, the BNE (Branch on result *not* equal to zero) was taken.

However, when this same instruction was executed the third time, the display showed:

```
Third
execution  →  1005 C9 03                    CMP   #$03
              A=03 X=00 Y=00 P=33 S=00
                              ↑
                             └P has changed
```

The Processor Status Register now holds 33.

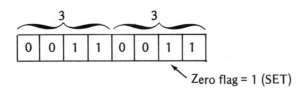

Zero flag = 1 (SET)

The value in the accumulator (03) is equal to 3. The result (03-03) does equal zero.

The branch (BNE) is *not* taken, and the execution of the program stops.

You can see that by looking at certain bits in the Processor Status Register, the computer can make decisions (such as the order in which instructions are executed) depending on certain conditions. This type of decision making adds great power to the capability of both the computer and the programmer.

Some instructions affect the status bits of the Processor Status Register and others do not. Here is a table of the instructions we have covered so far and the flags that they affect in the Processor Status Register.

Instruction	Status Bits Affected
PLA	Z,C
LDA	N,Z
ADC	N,V,Z,C
STA	none
RTS	none
CLC	C
LDX	N,Z
TXA	N,Z
INX	N,Z
CPX	N,Z,C
BNE	none
CMP	N,Z,C
SBC	N,V,Z,C
TAX	N,Z
SEC	C

Figure 5-2.   Effect of Instructions on Flag Bits

The following table shows the status flags that are affected by each 6502 instruction. X means that the flag is affected. The result will depend upon the condition, or status, resulting from the operation performed by the instruction. A one indicates that the flag is set. A zero indicates that a flag is reset.

Mnemonic Code	Operation Performed	Status Flags						
		N	V	B	D	I	Z	C
ADC	Add memory to accumulator with carry	X	X				X	X
AND	AND memory with accumulator	X					X	
ASL	Shift left one bit (memory or accum.)	X					X	X
BCC	Branch on carry clear (If C=0)							
BCS	Branch on carry set (If C=1)							
BEQ	Branch on result zero (If Z=1)							
BIT	Test bits in accumulator with memory	X	X				X	
BMI	Branch on result minus (If N=1)							
BNE	Branch on result not zero (If Z=0)							
BPL	Branch on result plus (If N=0)							
BRK	Force Break					1		
BVC	Branch on overflow clear (If V=0)							
BVS	Branch on overflow set (If V=1)							
CLC	Clear carry flag							0
CLD	Clear decimal mode				0			

Mnemonic Code	Operation Performed	N	V		B	D	I	Z	C
CLI	Clear interrupt disable flag						0		
CLV	Clear overflow flag		0						
CMP	Compare memory and accumulator	X						X	X
CPX	Compare memory and index X	X						X	X
CPY	Compare memory and index Y	X						X	X
DEC	Decrement memory by one							X	X
DEX	Decrement index X by one							X	X
DEY	Decrement index Y by one							X	X
EOR	Exclusive OR memory with accumulator							X	X
INC	Increment memory by one							X	X
INX	Increment index X by one							X	X
INY	Increment index Y by one							X	X
JMP	Jump to new location								
JSR	Jump to new location save rtn. add.								
LDA	Load accumulator from memory							X	X
LDX	Load index X from memory							X	X
LDY	Load index Y from memory							X	X
LSR	Shift right one bit (memory or accum.)	0						X	X
NOP	No operation								
ORA	OR memory with accumulator	X						X	
PHA	Push accumulator on stack								
PHP	Push processor status on stack								
PLA	Pull accumulator from stack							X	X
PLP	Pull processor status from stack	X	X	X	X	X	X	X	X
ROL	Rotate one bit left (mem. or accum.)	X						X	X
ROR	Rotate one bit right (mem. or accum.)	X						X	X
RTI	Return from interrupt	X	X	X	X	X	X	X	X
RTS	Return from subroutine								
SBC	Subtract memory and borrow from accum.	X	X					X	X
SEC	Set carry flag								1
SED	Set decimal mode					1			
SEI	Set interrupt disable flag						1		
STA	Store accumulator in memory								
STX	Store index X in memory								
STY	Store index Y in memory								
TAX	Transfer accumulator to index X	X						X	
TAY	Transfer accumulator to index Y	X						X	
TSX	Transfer stack pointer to index X	X						X	
TXA	Transfer index X to accumulator	X						X	
TXS	Transfer index X to stack pointer								
TYA	Transfer index Y to accumulator	X						X	

Flag abbreviations are:

N	Negative result flag	D	Decimal mode flag
V	Overflow flag	I	Interrupt disable flag
	Expansion flag (not labeled)	Z	Zero result flag
B	Break command flag	C	Carry flag

The Flags are up!

THE STACK POINTER REGISTER

Temporary storage is sometimes required to save current values of a register while it is being used for a second task. When that task is finished, the original value is replaced in the register. The microprocessor uses an area of RAM called a *stack* for this purpose. Values that are saved in this area are arranged like a stack of cards with each card having a value. Each value saved is placed on the top of the stack. When the values are retrieved, they are taken from the top of the stack also. The last value put on the stack is always the first value taken off.

Stack ⟨   Last on will be the first off

The Stack Pointer Register is a 16-bit register that keeps track of the memory address of the *top* of the stack.

Example:

Suppose the top of the stack is originally at address 01FF. If two data values are placed on the stack, the Stack Pointer Register would then contain the value 01FD.

Stack Pointer
originally
[01FF]

01FD	?	← Next value here
01FE	65	← 2nd value placed on
01FF	10	← 1st value placed on

Stack Pointer

now

the next location where data is to be placed

The process is reversed when data is taken off the stack. The stack pointer would be automatically incremented to point at 01FE and the value 65 returned. When ready to remove the value 03, the stack pointer would again be incremented and the 03 returned. The Stack Pointer Register would then contain 01FF again.

There are four machine language instructions that the programmer may use to move data on or off the stack. Data may be saved and retrieved from the Accumulator or the Processor Status Register.

1. PHA (PusH Acummulator on stack)
    Op Code = 48
        Implied mode
2. PHP (PusH Processor status on stack)
    Op Code = 08
        Implied mode
3. PLA (PulL Accumulator from stack)
    Op Code = 68
        Implied mode
4. PLP (PulL Processor status from stack)
    Op Code = 28
        Implied mode

ADDRESSING MODES

There are several different addressing modes used by the 6502 micropro-cessor. Some instructions are only used in one addressing mode. Others may be used in more than one mode. So far, we have only used three modes: the Imme-diate, the Implied, and the Relative.

The addressing modes may be classified into two types: Indexed and Non-Indexed. Let's first consider the Non-Indexed Addressing modes. They are the simplest to use and understand.

The Implied Addressing Mode

Instructions using Implied Addressing are one byte long. That byte con-tains the Op Code, which designates an operation that is internal to the micro-processor, and no operand is involved. Examples that we have used in this chap-ter are INX and TAX.

page 74   INX (Increment X register by one)
        Op Code E8
            Status flags effected: N and Z

page 76   TAX (Transfer Accumulator to X register)
             Op Code AA
             Status flags effected: N and Z

The Op Code totally defines the operation of Implied Addressing Instructions. Therefore, only one byte is needed to describe the operation. Instructions used in this mode are *not* used in any other mode.

The Immediate Addressing Mode

Instructions using the Immediate Addressing mode employ two bytes to describe the operation. The first byte contains the Op Code specifying the operation *and* the addressing mode. The second byte contains a constant value known at the time a program is being written. Putting these values directly in the program saves the programmer from loading them into memory and retrieving them when needed.

You have used the following Immediate Addressing mode instructions in Chapters 3, 4, and 5.

page 42   CPX   (Compare to X register)
             Op Code EO (If Immediate Addressing)
             Second byte OA (Value X is compared to)
             Status flags affected: N,Z and C

page 42   LDX   (Load the X register)
             Op Code A2 (If Immediate Addressing)
             Second byte 00 (Value loaded in X)
             Status flags affected: Z and C

page 57   LDA   (Load the Accumulator)
             Op Code A9 (If Immediate Addressing)
             Second byte 00 (Value loaded)
             Status flags affected: N and Z

page 57   ADC   (Add to Accumulator with carry)
             Op Code 69 (If Immediate Addressing)
             Second byte 01 (Value added)
             Status flags affected: N,Z,C and V

page 57   CMP   (Compare to Accumulator)
             Op Code C9 (If Immediate Addressing)
             Second byte 03 (Value accumulator is compared to)
             Status flags affected: N,Z and C

Immediate addressing is the simplest way to manipulate constants. All of the instructions used in this mode may also be used in other modes. The Op Code of the instruction will be different for each mode that it is used in so that the computer will know which mode is desired.

The Relative Addressing Mode

All of the branch instructions use this, and only this, mode. They are two-byte instructions. The Op Code occupies the first byte. The second byte contains a signed number that specifies the length of the branch (*if* the branch is taken). The second byte is ignored if the conditions existing do not require the branch to be taken. At the time the decision (to branch or not) is taken, the program counter is pointing at the *next* instruction. You have used one instruction in the Relative Addressing Mode, BNE.

> page 60   BNE   (Branch on result not equal to zero)
> Op Code DO
> Second byte FA (equivalent to –6: back 6 locations)
> Status flags affected: none

Branches are made, or not made, depending on the status of certain flags of the Processor Status Register (N,V,Z or C). Only branch instructions use this mode.

The Absolute Addressing Mode

Absolute Addressing Instructions contain three bytes: one for the Op Code and two for the address operand. The low-order address byte occupies the second byte, and the high-order address byte occupies the third byte. The programmer can therefore specify a full 16-bit address to access any memory location. It is considered to be the normal mode for addressing. You have used this mode in Chapter 2 with a STORE instruction (page 21). This mode will be used again in the next chapter.

Example:

> LDA (Load Accumulator)
> Op Code AD (If Absolute Addressing)
> Second byte F3 (low-order address)
> Third byte 10 (high-order address)
> Status flags affected: N and Z

This example would load the value that is contained in memory location 10F3 into the accumulator. The value held in 10F3 remains the same.

The Zero Page Addressing Mode

Zero Page instructions are two bytes long. The first byte contains the Op Code, and the second byte contains the low-order byte of the address operand. The high-order address byte is assumed by the microprocessor to be zero (therefore, its name). The zero page of memory runs from 0000 through 00FF. Each consecutive block of 256 locations is called a page of memory. The advantage of zero page instructions is the saving of one byte in the instruction. The time necessary to execute the instruction is therefore shorter than that of Absolute Addressing. The user should organize his use of memory so that the most frequently accessed memory is in the zero page. This cannot always be done because manufacturers of computers quite often use this memory in their operating system. We have not used any instructions in this mode yet.

Example:

LDA (Load the Accumulator)
Op Code A5 (If Zero Page Addressing)
Second byte 80 (low-order address byte)
Status flags affected: N and Z

This example would load the accumulator with the contents of memory location 0080.

We will hold off a discussion of Indexed Addressing modes until Chapter 8, where they are first used.

INSTRUCTION SET WITH ADDRESSING MODES

Mnemonic Code	Op Codes												
	Accumulator	*Immediate*	*Zero Page*	*Zero Page, X*	*Zero Page, Y*	*Absolute*	*Absolute, X*	*Absolute, Y*	*Implied*	*Relative*	*Indexed Indirect*	*Indirect Indexed*	*Indirect*
ADC	–	69	65	75	–	6D	7D	79	–	–	61	71	–
AND	–	29	25	35	–	2D	3D	39	–	–	21	31	–
ASL	0A	–	06	16	–	0E	1E	–	–	–	–	–	–
BCC	–	–	–	–	–	–	–	–	–	90	–	–	–
BCS	–	–	–	–	–	–	–	–	–	B0	–	–	–
BEQ	–	–	–	–	–	–	–	–	–	F0	–	–	–
BIT	–	–	24	–	–	2C	–	–	–	–	–	–	–
BMI	–	–	–	–	–	–	–	–	–	30	–	–	–
BNE	–	–	–	–	–	–	–	–	–	D0	–	–	–
BPL	–	–	–	–	–	–	–	–	–	10	–	–	–
BRK	–	–	–	–	–	–	–	–	00	–	–	–	–
BVC	–	–	–	–	–	–	–	–	–	50	–	–	–
BVS	–	–	–	–	–	–	–	–	–	70	–	–	–
CLC	–	–	–	–	–	–	–	–	18	–	–	–	–
CLD	–	–	–	–	–	–	–	–	D8	–	–	–	–
CLI	–	–	–	–	–	–	–	–	58	–	–	–	–
CLV	–	–	–	–	–	–	–	–	B8	–	–	–	–

Mnemonic Code	Op Codes												
	Accumulator	Immediate	Zero Page	Zero Page, X	Zero Page, Y	Absolute	Absolute, X	Absolute, Y	Implied	Relative	Indexed Indirect	Indirect Indexed	Indirect
CMP	–	C9	C5	D5	–	CD	DD	D9	–	–	C1	D1	–
CPX	–	E0	E4	–	–	EC	–	–	–	–	–	–	–
CPY	–	C0	C4	–	–	CC	–	–	–	–	–	–	–
DEC	–	–	C6	D6	–	CE	DE	–	–	–	–	–	–
DEX	–	–	–	–	–	–	–	–	CA	–	–	–	–
DEY	–	–	–	–	–	–	–	–	88	–	–	–	–
EOR	–	49	45	55	–	4D	5D	59	–	–	41	51	–
INC	–	–	E6	F6	–	EE	FE	–	–	–	–	–	–
INX	–	–	–	–	–	–	–	–	E8	–	–	–	–
INY	–	–	–	–	–	–	–	–	C8	–	–	–	–
JMP	–	–	–	–	–	4C	–	–	–	–	–	–	6C
JSR	–	–	–	–	–	20	–	–	–	–	–	–	–
LDA	–	A9	A5	B5	–	AD	BD	B9	–	–	A1	B1	–
LDX	–	A2	A6	–	B6	AE	–	BE	–	–	–	–	–
LDY	–	A0	A4	B4	–	AC	BC	–	–	–	–	–	–
LSR	4A	–	46	56	–	4E	5E	–	–	–	–	–	–
NOP	–	–	–	–	–	–	–	–	EA	–	–	–	–
ORA	–	09	05	15	–	0D	1D	19	–	–	01	11	–
PHA	–	–	–	–	–	–	–	–	48	–	–	–	–
PHP	–	–	–	–	–	–	–	–	08	–	–	–	–
PLA	–	–	–	–	–	–	–	–	68	–	–	–	–
PLP	–	–	–	–	–	–	–	–	28	–	–	–	–
ROL	2A	–	26	36	–	2E	3E	–	–	–	–	–	–
ROR	6A	–	66	76	–	6E	7E	–	–	–	–	–	–
RTI	–	–	–	–	–	–	–	–	40	–	–	–	–
RTS	–	–	–	–	–	–	–	–	60	–	–	–	–
SBC	–	E9	E5	F5	–	ED	FD	F9	–	–	E1	F1	–
SEC	–	–	–	–	–	–	–	–	38	–	–	–	–
SED	–	–	–	–	–	–	–	–	F8	–	–	–	–
SEI	–	–	–	–	–	–	–	–	78	–	–	–	–
STA	–	–	85	95	–	8D	9D	99	–	–	81	91	–
STX	–	–	86	–	96	8E	–	–	–	–	–	–	–
STY	–	–	84	94	–	8C	–	–	–	–	–	–	–
TAX	–	–	–	–	–	–	–	–	AA	–	–	–	–
TAY	–	–	–	–	–	–	–	–	A8	–	–	–	–
TSX	–	–	–	–	–	–	–	–	BA	–	–	–	–
TXA	–	–	–	–	–	–	–	–	8A	–	–	–	–
TXS	–	–	–	–	–	–	–	–	9A	–	–	–	–
TYA	–	–	–	–	–	–	–	–	98	–	–	–	–

SUMMARY

The flexibility of the 6502 microprocessor used in the Atari 400/800 computers is achieved through a variety of addressing modes and special-purpose registers.

The registers discussed in this chapter include:

- Accumulator (A register)—Most operations performed on data take place in this register.
- X Index Register—Used as a scratch pad or as an index in some addressing modes.
- Y Index Register—same function as X Index Register.
- Processor Status Register (P register)—Contains the microprocessor's status as each instruction is executed.
- Stack Pointer Register (S register)—Contains the memory location of the top of the stack.

The addressing modes discussed include:

- Implied—One-byte instructions that need no operand.
- Immediate—The first byte specifies the operation; the operand (second byte) is a one-byte data item.
- Relative—Used for branch instructions; first byte specifies the kind of branch; the one byte operand tells how far and in what direction to branch.
- Absolute—A three-byte instruction; first byte specifies the operation; the other two bytes give the operand that consists of a memory address to be used.
- Zero Page—Similar to Absolute Addressing, but only a single-byte operand is necessary for the memory address to be used.

EXERCISES

1. How many *bits* of information can be contained in the accumulator? _____ bits
2. Name the two index registers.
   _____ and _____
3. The status flags are contained in which register?
   _____ _____ register
4. The register into which data is loaded, stored from, and in which arithmetic operations are performed is called: _____

Question 5 through 8 refer to the following program:

```
10    *=$1050
20    LDX #0
30 LOOP INX
40    CPX #2
50    BNE LOOP
60    END
```

5. Which index register is used in the program? _____

6. Which status flag is used to determine if a branch is taken? _____

7. What values will appear in the index register as the program is executed?

_____ _____ _____

8. What will be the starting address of the machine language program when it is assembled? _____

9. The assembler cartridge's Writer/Editor command to display the assembly language program on the video screen is: _____
(NEW, LIST, RUN)

10. The bits of the Processor Status Register are labeled as shown:

N	V		B	D	I	Z	C

   (a) Bit B_1 contains the _____ flag.

   (b) Bit B_7 contains the _____ flag.

   (c) The Carry flag is contained in bit _____.

11. When using the stack, the Stack Pointer Register contains the memory address of the top of the stack. The last item placed on the stack will be the _____item removed from the stack.
      (first, last)

12. How many bytes are used by an Implied Address instruction? _____

13. What addressing mode is used by Branch instructions? _____

14. Which instruction is shorter (fewer bytes):

   Absolute or Zero Page? _____

ANSWERS

1. 8 bits

2. X and Y

3. Processor Status Register

4. The accumulator (or A register)

5. X

6. Zero (or Zero flag)

7. 0,1,2 (or 00000000,00000001,00000010 binary)

8. 1050 (hex)

9. LIST

10. (a) Z (or Zero flag)

    (b) N (or Negative flag)

    (c) B_0

11. First

12. 1 (one)

13. Relative

14. Zero Page

Chapter 6

Branching Out

In Chapters 3, 4, and 5 we have used a branch instruction (BNE) to perform a program loop. Branch instructions are two-byte instructions which use the Relative Addressing mode. That is, the address to which the branch is to be taken is calculated *relative* to the current position of the *program counter*. The program counter (see page 000) is used as a pointer to designate where the microprocessor will obtain the instruction that is to be executed following the instruction that is currently being executed. It is always one instruction ahead of the computer execution.

Example:

	Memory	Op Code	Instruction
As this instruction → is being executed,	1008	D0	BNE
	1009	F9	
Program Counter points ⟹ here	100A	00	BRK

Therefore, the branch is taken relative to the program counter (or one memory location beyond the second byte of the branch instruction). The operand (second byte—F9 in this example) used with the branch instruction tells how far and in what direction the branch should be taken.

When used as the operand in a branch instruction such as BNE, all hex values from 01 through 7F cause a branch *forward* from the current position of the program counter. The following instruction would cause a branch *forward* from memory location 100A (where the program counter points as the BNE instruction is executed) to hexadecimal memory location 1012 (100A+8).

1008	D0	BNE	08
1009	08		

An example of the above as used in a section of a program follows:

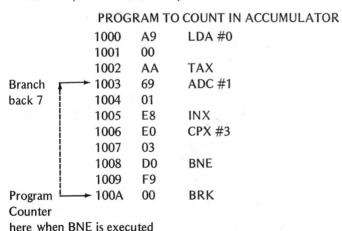

	1006	E0	CPX 03	Compare the value of the
	1007	03		X register with 03 hex.
	1008	D0	BNE 08	Branch, if Y is not equal to
Program	1009	08	'	03, forward 8 steps.
counter	100A	'	'	
starts	100B	'	'	
here	100C	'	'	
	100D	'	'	
	100E	'	'	
Branch	100F	'	'	
forward	1010	'	'	
8 steps	1011	'	'	
if X	1012	'	'	
not=03	1013	'	'	
	1014	'	'	

All hex values from 80 through FF are used by branch instructions as backward (or negative) branches. In the "Program to Count in Accumulator" (Chapter 5) the instruction used is:

1008	D0	BNE LOOP	The assembler looked for the label LOOP and counted back to see where to find it.
1009	F9		Branch, if X is not equal to 03, backward 7 steps.

The branch is made backward (or in the negative direction) since F9 is between 80 and FF. Counting back 7 steps from location 100A puts the branch destination at 1003, the start of the loop.

PROGRAM TO COUNT IN ACCUMULATOR

		1000	A9	LDA #0
		1001	00	
		1002	AA	TAX
Branch		1003	69	ADC #1
back 7		1004	01	
		1005	E8	INX
		1006	E0	CPX #3
		1007	03	
		1008	D0	BNE
		1009	F9	
Program		100A	00	BRK

Counter
here when BNE is executed

We will not go into the method used by the computer to determine the values of negative numbers. Instead, we will provide tables to determine the operand used with the branch. The assembler takes care of these details if you provide it with appropriate labels.

Remember that forward branches will use an operand in the range of 1 through 7F, and backward branches will use an operand in the range of 80 through FF.

EXAMPLES USING FORWARD BRANCHES

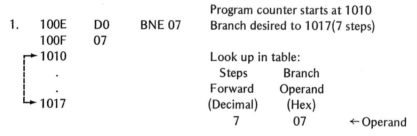

1.   100E   D0   BNE 07   Program counter starts at 1010
      100F   07   Branch desired to 1017 (7 steps)

      ┌─► 1010   Look up in table:
      │   ·   Steps   Branch
      │   ·   Forward   Operand
      └─► 1017   (Decimal)   (Hex)
                                  7   07   ← Operand

If condition tested is not equal to zero,
branch forward to 1017 (1010+7 steps).

2.   1010   D0   BNE 1F   Program counter starts at 1010
      1009   1F   Branch desired to 102F (31 decimal steps)

      ┌─► 1010   ·
      │   ·   ·   Look up in table:
      │   ·   ·   Steps   Branch
      └─► 102F   ·   Forward   Operand
                              (Decimal)   (Hex)
                                  31   1F   ← Operand

If condition tested is not equal to zero,
branch forward to 102F (1010+1F hex steps).

3.   100E   D0   BNE 77   Program counter starts at 1010
      100F   77   Branch desired to 1087 (119 decimal steps)

      ┌─► 1010   ·
      │   ·   ·   Look up in table:
      │   ·   ·   Steps   Branch
      └─► 1087   ·   Forward   Operand
                              (Decimal)   (Hex)
                                  119   77   ← Operand

If condition tested is not equal to zero,
branch forward to 1087 (1010+77 hex steps).

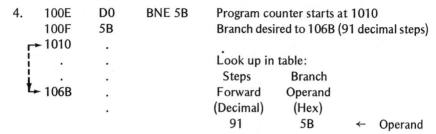

4. 100E   D0   BNE 5B   Program counter starts at 1010
    100F   5B   Branch desired to 106B (91 decimal steps)
    1010   .
           .   .   Look up in table:
           .   .   Steps   Branch
    106B   .   Forward   Operand
           .   (Decimal)   (Hex)
                                 91   5B   ← Operand

If condition tested is not equal to zero,
branch forward to 106B (1010+5B hex steps).

EXAMPLES USING BACKWARD BRANCHES

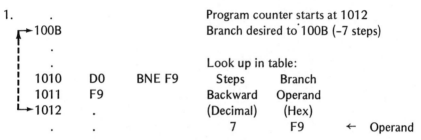

1.   .   Program counter starts at 1012
    100B   Branch desired to 100B (-7 steps)
      .
      .   Look up in table:
    1010   D0   BNE F9   Steps   Branch
    1011   F9   Backward   Operand
    1012   .   (Decimal)   (Hex)
      .   .   7   F9   ← Operand

If condition tested is not equal to zero,
branch backward to 100B (1012-7 steps).

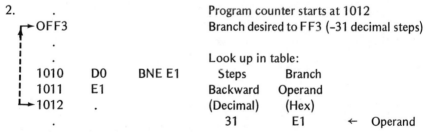

2.   .   Program counter starts at 1012
    0FF3   Branch desired to FF3 (-31 decimal steps)
      .
      .   Look up in table:
    1010   D0   BNE E1   Steps   Branch
    1011   E1   Backward   Operand
    1012   .   (Decimal)   (Hex)
      .   31   E1   ← Operand

If condition tested is not equal to zero,
branch backward to FF3 (1012-1F hex steps).

3.   .   Program counter starts at 1012
    0F9B   Branch desired to F9B (-119 decimal steps)
      .
      .   Look up in table:
    1010   D0   BNE 89   Steps   Branch
    1011   89   Backward   Operand
    1012   .   (Decimal)   (Hex)
      .   .   119   89   ← Operand

If condition tested is not equal to zero,
branch backward to F9B (1012-77 hex steps).

TABLE TO DETERMINE FORWARD BRANCHES

Steps Forward (Decimal)	Branch Operand (Hex)	Steps Forward (Decimal)	Branch Operand (Hex)	Steps Forward (Decimal)	Branch Operand (Hex)
1	01	49	31	97	61
2	02	50	32	98	62
3	03	51	33	99	63
4	04	52	34	100	64
5	05	53	35	101	65
6	06	54	36	102	66
7	07	55	37	103	67
8	08	56	38	104	68
9	09	57	39	105	69
10	0A	58	3A	106	6A
11	0B	59	3B	107	6B
12	0C	60	3C	108	6C
13	0D	61	3D	109	6D
14	0E	62	3E	110	6E
15	0F	63	3F	111	6F
16	10	64	40	112	70
17	11	65	41	113	71
18	12	66	42	114	72
19	13	67	43	115	73
20	14	68	44	116	74
21	15	69	45	117	75
22	16	70	46	118	76
23	17	71	47	119	77
24	18	72	48	120	78
25	19	73	49	121	79
26	1A	74	4A	122	7A
27	1B	75	4B	123	7B
28	1C	76	4C	124	7C
29	1D	77	4D	125	7D
30	1E	78	4E	126	7E
31	1F	79	4F	127	7F
32	20	80	50		
33	21	81	51		
34	22	82	52		
35	23	83	53		
36	24	84	54		
37	25	85	55		
38	26	86	56		
39	27	87	57		
40	28	88	58		
41	29	89	59		
42	2A	90	5A		
43	2B	91	5B		
44	2C	92	5C		
45	2D	93	5D		
46	2E	94	5E		
47	2F	95	5F		
48	30	96	60		

Figure 6-1. Forward Branches

TABLE TO DETERMINE BACKWARD BRANCHES

Steps Backward (Decimal)	Branch Operand (Hex)	Steps Backward (Decimal)	Branch Operand (Hex)	Steps Backward (Decimal)	Branch Operand (Hex)
1	FF	49	CF	97	9F
2	FE	50	CE	98	9E
3	FD	51	CD	99	9D
4	FC	52	CC	100	9C
5	FB	53	CB	101	9B
6	FA	54	CA	102	9A
7	F9	55	C9	103	99
8	F8	56	C8	104	98
9	F7	57	C7	105	97
10	F6	58	C6	106	96
11	F5	59	C5	107	95
12	F4	60	C4	108	94
13	F3	61	C3	109	93
14	F2	62	C2	110	92
15	F1	63	C1	111	91
16	F0	64	C0	112	90
17	EF	65	BF	113	8F
18	EE	66	BE	114	8E
19	ED	67	BD	115	8D
20	EC	68	BC	116	8C
21	EB	69	BB	117	8B
22	EA	70	BA	118	8A
23	E9	71	B9	119	89
24	E8	72	B8	120	88
25	E7	73	B7	121	87
26	E6	74	B6	122	86
27	E5	75	B5	123	85
28	E4	76	B4	124	84
29	E3	77	B3	125	83
30	E2	78	B2	126	82
31	E1	79	B1	127	81
32	E0	80	B0	128	80
33	DF	81	AF		
34	DE	82	AE		
35	DD	83	AD		
36	DC	84	AC		
37	DB	85	AB		
38	DA	86	AA		
39	D9	87	A9		
40	D8	88	A8		
41	D7	89	A7		
42	D6	90	A6		
43	D5	91	A5		
44	D4	92	A4		
45	D3	93	A3		
46	D2	94	A2		
47	D1	95	A1		
48	D0	96	A0		

Figure 6-2. Backward Branches

4.   .   Program counter starts at 1012

┌─ 0FB7   Branch desired to FB7 (–91 decimal steps)

| .

| .   Look up in table:

| 1010   D0   BNE A5   Steps   Branch

| 1011   A5   Backward   Operand

└─ 1012   .   (Decimal)   (Hex)

        .   .   91   A5

If condition tested is not equal to zero,
branch backward to FB7 (1012–5B hex steps).

NOTE—All of the above calculations were performed with hex numbers. Hexadecimal subtraction will be discussed in Chapter 9. The table in Figure
6-2 will give you the necessary operand for backward branches.

All branch instructions, listed in the following table, use the Relative
Addressing mode. The status flags that determine the condition on which the
branch is taken, or not taken, are given in the table.

Mnemonic Code	Instruction	Status Flag	Conditions for Branch
BCC	Branch on Carry Clear	C	0
BCS	Branch on Carry Set	C	1
BEQ	Branch on result zero	Z	1
BMI	Branch on result minus	N	1
BNE	Branch on result not zero	Z	0
BPL	Branch on result positive	N	0
BVC	Branch on overflow clear	V	0
BVS	Branch on overflow set	V	1

Figure 6-3. Status Flags for Branches

In order to demonstrate some of the branch instructions, we will write
some short demonstration programs that perform arithmetic operations.

USING THE CARRY FLAG 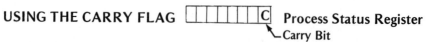 Process Status Register
Carry Bit

Suppose you were using the machine language subroutine on page 39,
and you input the decimal numbers 123 and 133. The result of their sum would
be displayed as zero because the result is too large to be contained in one byte.
An extra bit is needed to express the true result.

The sum of that problem:

Decimal		Binary
123	=	01111011
133	=	10000101

Sum = 1   00000000

extra   8 bits displayed

When an extra bit (as in this example) occurs from the addition of two 8-bit numbers, the computer automatically sets the carry flag (C=1). You can verify this by using the Atari Assembler Cartridge to enter the following program.

```
EDIT
10    *=$1000
20    CLC             ← Clear the carry flag
30    LDA #$7B        ← Load hex 7B (decimal 123)
40    ADC #$85        ← Add hex 85 (decimal 133)
50    END
■
```

Then assemble the program by typing: ASM

```
EDIT
10    *=$1000
20    CLC
30    LDA #$7B
40    ADC #$85
50    FND
ASM
0000            10       *= $1000

1000    18      20       CLC

1001    A97B    30       LDA #$7B

1003    6985    40       ADC #$85

                50 END

EDIT
■
```

Notice the symbols (# and $) used with the operands in lines 30 and 40 of the **Source Program** (the Assembly Language program). The # symbol tells the computer that the LDA and ADC instructions are to be used in the Immediate mode. The $ symbol tells the computer that the numbers in the operand are to be treated as hexadecimal values. The symbols are a necessary part of the assembly language instruction.

Enter the **Debugger Program** and trace the program. In this way, you can watch the changes in the Processor Status Register (P) where the status flags are stored. You will want to keep your eye on the Carry bit (flag) in the Processor Status Register before and after the add instruction is used.

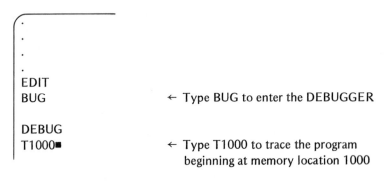

```
EDIT
BUG                          ← Type BUG to enter the DEBUGGER

DEBUG
T1000■                       ← Type T1000 to trace the program
                               beginning at memory location 1000
```

```
1000    18              CLC
  A=00 X=00 Y=00 P=B0 S=00
1001    A9  7B          LDA #$7B
  A=7B X=00 Y=00 P=30 S=00
1003    69  85          ADC #$85
  A=00 X=00 Y=00 P=33 S=00
1005    00              BRK
  A=00 X=00 Y=00 P=33 S=00
DEBUG
■
```

Notice that at step 1003 the accumulator changed to zero, and the Processor Status Register changed from 30 to 33. The accumulator tells us that the sum is zero, but consider what the P register shows.

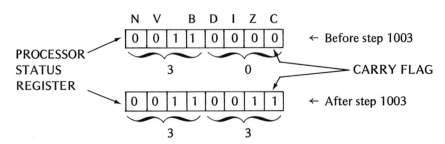

We can consider the result to be a combination of the carry bit and the value in the accumulator.

In Hexadecimal

$$1 + 0 \ 0 \ = \ 100$$

carry bit   in accumulator

In decimal this would be 256 + 0 = 256

By expanding our program, we can store the results in memory by making use of the the Branch on Carry Clear (BCC) instruction. Use the NEW command to clear the EDIT Buffer.

Using the **Writer/Editor Program** of the Assembly Cartridge:

```
EDIT
10    *=$1000
20    CLC
30    LDA #$00              Load and store 0 in 1050
40    STA $1050
50    LDA #$7D          (7x16)+13 = 125 decimal
60    ADC #$A4          (10x16)+4 = 164 decimal
70    STA $1051            Sum = 289 decimal
80    BCC END
90    INC $1050                = 256 + 32 + 1
100   END
■                        =   1    2    1 hex
```

stored in 1050   stored in 1051

The program adds two hex numbers and stores the low 8 bits from the accumulator into memory location 1051. If there was a carry, memory location 1050 will be incremented at line 90. If no carry is made, the instruction (BCC) at line 80 will cause the computer to skip over the INC instruction at line 90 and go to the end of the program. Thus, memory location 1050 will contain the extra bit when a carry has been made but will be zero if no carry was made. The combination of memory locations 1050 and 1051 will provide the complete result. Assemble the program and execute it. Then look at the results:

            Assembly
Type: ASM

```
0000              10          *= $1000

1000   18         20          CLC

1001   A900       30          LDA #$00
```

1003	8D5010	40	STA $1050
1006	A97D	50	LDA #$7D
1008	69A4	60	ADC #$A4
100A	8D5110	70	STA $1051
100D	9003	80	BCC END
100F	EE5010	90	INC $1050
		0100 END	

EDIT
■

Notice that the STA operand and the INC operand take two bytes for the address involved. The $ sign once again indicates a hexadecimal value. The Branch on Carry Clear operand shows a forward branch of 3 steps from 100F to 1012 where the program stops.

This is the first time you have used the INC instruction. It is used to increment by one the value in the specified memory location. It is similar to the INX instruction (increment the X register) that you used earlier.

Example:

INC (Increment memory)
    Op code EE (If Absolute mode addressing)
    Second byte 50 (Least significant address byte)
    Third byte 10 (Most significant address byte)
      Status flags affected: Z and C
        DEBUG and Execute

Type: BUG

.
.
BUG

DEBUG
■

Type: T1000 (to trace the program)

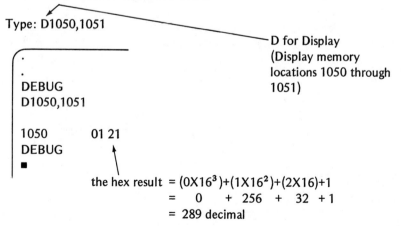

```
DEBUG
T1000
1000    18              CLC
  A=D7 X=00 Y=00 P=B0 S=00
1001    00              LDA  #$00
  A=00 X=00 Y=00 P=32 S=00
1003    8D 50 10        STA  $1050
  A=00 X=00 Y=00 P=32 S=00
1006    A9 7D           LDA  #$7D
  A=7D X=00 Y=00 P=30 S=00
1008    69 A4           ADC  #$A4
  A=21 X=00 Y=00 P=31 S=00
100A    8D 51 10        STA  $1051
  A=21 X=00 Y=00 P=31 S=00          Carry is set,
100D    90 03           BCC  $1012  ──── no branch
  A=21 X=00 Y=00 P=31 S=00                          C flag
100F    EE 50 10        INC  $1050  P 00110001
  A=21 X=00 Y=00 P=31 S=00
1012    00              BRK              3   1
  A=21 X=00 Y=00 P=31 S=00
DEBUG
■
```

Notice that a branch was *not* made at 100D (the Carry flag was not clear, it was set). Therefore the memory location 1050 was incremented at line 100F.

Check Results

To check the results, you will want to display the memory locations 1050 and 1051 to verify that the answer is correct.

Type: D1050,1051

D for Display
(Display memory
locations 1050 through
1051)

```
    .
    .
DEBUG
D1050,1051

1050        01 21
DEBUG
■
```

the hex result = $(0 \times 16^3) + (1 \times 16^2) + (2 \times 16) + 1$
              = 0 + 256 + 32 + 1
              = 289 decimal

We could use the Branch on Carry Set (BCS) instruction in the previous program instead of the Branch on Carry Clear.

Using BCC			Using BCS	
010	*=$1000		010	*=$1000
020	CLC		020	CLC
030	LDA #$0		030	LDA #$0
040	STA $1050		040	STA $1050
050	LDA #$7D		050	LDA #$7D
060	ADC #$A4		060	ADC #$A4
070	STA $1051		070	STA $1051
080	BCC END		080	BCS SET
090	INC $1050	change	090	JMP END
100	END		100	SET INC $1050
			110	END

The result of these two programs would be the same. The program using BCS would *jump* to the END at line 90 if the Carry flag had *not* been set. It would *branch* from line 80 to line 100 if a carry *had* been set.

The JMP instruction at line 90 in the second program is similar to a branch instruction. However the jump is made regardless of any condition. Therefore it is called an *unconditional* instruction. It is used here in the Absolute Addressing mode.

> All BRANCH instructions are dependent on some condition expressed by the status flags in the Processor Status Register.

> All JUMP instructions are unconditional.

USING THE ZERO FLAG ⬚⬚⬚⬚⬚⬚⬚Z⬚ Processor Status Register
↖ Zero bit

In Chapter 4, you used a program which counted from 1 through FF. The counting loop was accomplished by comparing the value in the accumulator with FF and using the Branch on result Not Equal zero (BNE). This was the assembler program:

10	*=$1000
20	CLC
30	LDA #0
40	LOOP ADC #1
50	CMP #$FF
60	BNE LOOP
70	END

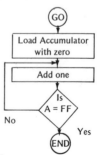

The companion instruction to BNE is BEQ (Branch on result EQual to zero). The counting program could be written to use the BEQ instruction in the following way:

10	*$1000
20	CLC
30	LDA #0
40	LOOP ADC #1
50	CMP #$FF
60	BEQ END
70	JMP LOOP
80	END

Use the assembler to enter and *trace* each program. You can see from the flowcharts that the first program (using BNE) is more straightforward. However, you do have the option of using either instruction (BNE or BEQ). In some programs the BEQ instruction would be the best choice.

If you time the traces of the two programs you will find that the first program is a little faster. You can see by the printout of the traces that one more instruction must be executed each time the second program passes through the counting loop.

Trace of BNE program:

Video Display at the end of the trace:

```
   1007    D0 FA          BNE   $1003
      A=FD X=00 Y=00 P=B0 S=00
   1003    69 01          ADC   #$01
      A=FE X=00 Y=00 P=B0 S=00        A=FE    P=B0
   1005    C9 FF          CMP   #$FF
      A=FE X=00 Y=00 P=B0 S=00      Branch is taken
   1007    D0 FA          BNE   $1003  back to 1003
      A=FE X=00 Y=00 P=B0 S=00
   1003    69 01          ADC   #$01
      A=FF X=00 Y=00 P=B0 S=00
   1005    C9 FF          CMP   #$FF   A=FF    P=33
      A=FF X=00 Y=00 P=33 S=00
   1007    D0 FA          BNE   $1003  Branch is not taken
      A=FF X=00 Y=00 P=33 S=00        Program ends
   1009    00             BRK
      A=FF X=00 Y=00 P=33 S=00
   DEBUG
```

3 instructions in this loop

This trace took approximately 2.3 minutes.
Notice the Processor Status Register after the Compare instruction:

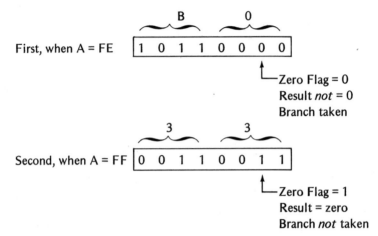

First, when A = FE

B				0			
1	0	1	1	0	0	0	0

└─Zero Flag = 0
Result *not* = 0
Branch taken

Second, when A = FF

3				3			
0	0	1	1	0	0	1	1

└─Zero Flag = 1
Result = zero
Branch *not* taken

Trace of BEQ Program:

Video Display at the end of the trace:

```
                    .
                    .
                    .
4           1009    4C 03 10        JMP     $1003
instructions        A=FD X=00 Y=00 P=B0 S=00
in this     1003    69 01           ADC    #$01
loop                A=FE X=00 Y=00 P=B0 S=00
            1005    C9 FF           CMP    #$FF
                    A=FE X=00 Y=00 P=B0 S=00      ←First A=FE
            1007    F0 05           BEQ END
                    A=FE X=00 Y=00 P=B0 S=00      ⟩ Branch not taken
            1009    4C 03 10        JMP     $1003
                    A=FE X=00 Y=00 P=B0 S=00
            1003    69 01           ADC    #$01
                    A=FF X=00 Y=00 P=B0 S=00
            1005    C9 FF           CMP    #$FF
                    A=FF X=00 Y=00 P=33 S=00      ← Second A=FF
            1007    F0 05           BEQ END
                    A=FF X=00 Y=00 P=33 S=00      ⟩ Branch is taken
            100C    00              BRK             to the end
                    A=FF X=00 Y=00 P=33 S=00
            DEBUG
            ■
```

This trace took approximately 3.1 minutes.

Once again, notice the Processor Status Register after the Compare instruction:

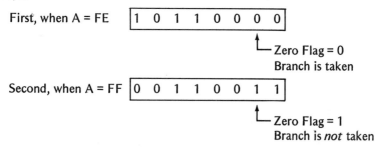

First, when A = FE | 1 | 0 | 1 | 1 | 0 | 0 | 0 | 0 |

              Zero Flag = 0
              Branch is taken

Second, when A = FF | 0 | 0 | 1 | 1 | 0 | 0 | 1 | 1 |

              Zero Flag = 1
              Branch is *not* taken

The BEQ program took a longer time to trace than the BNE program. This difference in timing would not be noticed if the program is run in the normal manner. However, in the trace mode, the time for printing the extra step is noticeable.

USING THE NEGATIVE FLAG 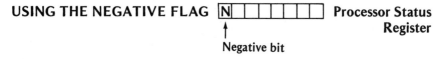 **Processor Status Register**

Negative bit

Once again, let's use a variation of the counting program to see how some branch instructions decide whether a number is positive or negative. We'll first use the Branch on result Plus (BPL) instruction. The N (negative) flag is reset to zero for positive numbers and is set to 1 for negative numbers when certain instructions are executed. If the Negative flag has been reset to zero, the BPL instruction will cause a branch to be taken (because the result is positive). If the Negative flag has been set to 1 (result negative), the branch will *not* be taken.

BRANCH ON RESULT PLUS DEMONSTRATION

Using the assembler cartridge, enter the following program in the Writer/Editor mode. Type NEW to clear the last program:

```
10      *=$1000
20      CLC
30      LDA #0
40      LOOP ADC #1
50      BPL LOOP
60      END
```

Assemble the demonstration program. Then enter the Debugger Mode and trace the program.

```
      .
      .
      .
ASM
0000              10            *= $1000

1000 18           20            CLC

1001 A900         30            LDA #$00

1003 6901         40 LOOP       ADC #$01

1005 10FA         50            BPL LOOP

                  60 END

EDIT
BUG                             ← Enter Debugger

DEBUG
T1000                           ← Trace the program
```

The end of the trace looks like this:

```
      .
      .
      .
1003    69 01            ADC   #01
   A=7F X=00 Y=00 P=30 S=00
1005    10 FA            BPL  $1003  ← Branch back to 1003
   A=7F X=00 Y=00 P=30 S=00
1003    69 01            ADC  #$01
   A=80 X=00 Y=00 P=F0 S=00         ← Notice change in P
1005    10 FA            BPL  $1003     when A = 80
   A=80 X=00 Y=00 P=F0 S=00
1007    00               BRK           ← Branch not taken
   A=80 X=00 Y=00 P=F0 S=00
DEBUG
■
```

Notice that the branch loop was executed until the value in the accumulator reached 80. This was the first negative value reached.

| 1 | 1 | 1 | 1 | 0 | 0 | 0 | 0 |

Process Status Register

↑
N set to 1

Negative values can be more dramatically seen by starting with zero in the accumulator and subtracting one each time through a loop.

Operation	Result	Signed Decimal Equivalent
0 - 1	FF	-1
FF - 1	FE	-2
FE - 1	FD	-3
FD - 1	FC	-4
.	.	.
.	.	.
etc	.	.
.	.	.
.	.	.
83 - 1	82	-126
82 - 1	81	-127
81 - 1	80	-128

You might think of 8-bit signed numbers as locations on a large number wheel rather than the usual number line. Then they would look like this.

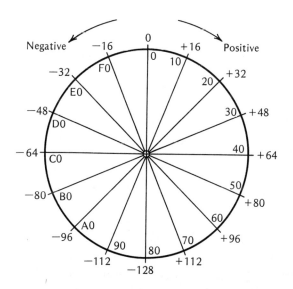

Figure 6-4. Signed Number Wheel. Hex Values Inside;
Decimal Equivalents Outside

To demonstrate the subtraction of one from the accumulator, we'll use the Branch on result MInus (BMI) to create a loop. The carry bit is used in subtraction in the borrowing process. When using addition, we *cleared* the Carry bit before performing the operation. In subtraction, we must *set* the carry bit before performing the operation. Here is the program as entered during the assembler's Writer/Editor mode.

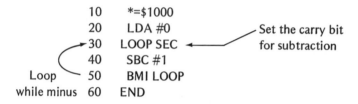

```
        10      *=$1000
        20      LDA #0          Set the carry bit
       →30      LOOP SEC ←      for subtraction
        40      SBC #1
Loop    50      BMI LOOP
while minus  60  END
```

Assemble the program. Then enter the Debug mode and single step through the first part of the program.

```
ASM
0000              10              *= $1000

1000   A900       20              LDA #$00

1002   38         30 LOOP         SEC

1003   E901       40              SBC #$01

1005   30FB       50              BMI LOOP

                  60 END

EDIT
BUG                       ← Enter Debugger

DEBUG
S1000                     ←      Single step starting at 1000
```

```
DEBUG
S1000                              ← First step
1000    A9 00        LDA    #$00       Load 0 in accumulator
  A=00 X=00 Y=00 P=33 S=00
```

```
DEBUG
S                                              ← Type S and press RETURN
1002    38              SEC                       Set Carry flag
   A=00 X=00 Y=00 P=33 S=00
DEBUG
S                                              ← Third step
1003    E9 01           SBC     #$01             Subtract one
   A=FF X=00 Y=00 P=B0 S=00                       A=FF; Negative flag on
DEBUG
S                                              ← Fourth step
1005    30 FB           BMI     $1002            Branch if negative
   A=FF X=00 Y=00 P=B0 S=00
DEBUG
S                                              ← Fifth step
1002    38              SEC                       Set Carry flag
   A=FF X=00 Y=00 P=B1 S=00
DEBUG
S                                              ← Sixth step
1003    E9 01           SBC     #$01             Subtract one again
   A=FE X=00 Y=00 P=B1 S=00
DEBUG
S                                              ← Seventh step
1005    30 FB           BMI     $1002            Branch if negative
   A=FE X=00 Y=00 P=B1 S=00
DEBUG
S                                              ← Eighth step
1002    38              SEC                       Set Carry flag
   A=FE X=00 Y=00 P=B1 S=00
DEBUG
■
```

STOP at this point

You can see that this will go on for some time before we finally reach a non-negative number. You can also see that the computer considers FF and FE as negative values and therefore branches back to subtract again. It will branch back until the accumulator reaches 7F. By looking at the Signed Number Wheel in Figure 6-4, you will find that 80 is interpreted as a negative value (–128 decimal). However, 7F is interpreted as positive (+127 decimal). Therefore, the branch will not be taken at that point.

Instead of plodding on through all the negative integers up to and including –128, change to the Trace mode to finish up the program. After the last DE-

BUG prompt, type T1000 and press RETURN. Now the computer will trace through the program, and you can see the END result.

As seen on the display:

```
   .
   .
   .
1005    30 FB          BMI  $1002
   A=80 X=00 Y=00 P=B1 S=00           ← 80 still considered
1002    38             SEC              negative—branch
   A=80 X=00 Y=00 P=B1 S=00
1003    E9 01          SBC  #$01
   A=7F X=00 Y=00 P=71 S=00           ← Negative flag off (P = 71)
1005    30 FB          BMI  $1002
   A=7F X=00 Y=00 P=71 S=00           ← 7F considered positive—
1007    00             BRK              no branch taken
   A=7F X=00 Y=00 P=71 S=00
DEBUG
■
```

THE OVERFLOW FLAG

Two branch instructions BVC (Branch on oVerflow Clear) and BVS (Branch on oVerflow Set) can also change the normal sequential operation of a machine language program. If you are not performing arithmetic with signed numbers, the Overflow flag may be completely ignored. We will discuss arithmetic with signed numbers in Chapter 9.

Processor Status Register.

overflow flag

SUMMARY

This chapter discussed branch instructions—what they are and how they are used. You learned that:

- All branch instructions are made in the Relative Addressing mode;
- Branch instructions cause a branch when a specified condition is true;
- The Program Counter is moved relative to its current position when a branch is taken;
- The second byte of a branch instruction tells how far and in what direction (forward or backward) the Program Counter is moved;

- Forward branches are taken when the second byte of the branch instruction is in the range of 1 through 7F;
- Backward branches are taken when the second byte of the branch instruction is in the range of 80 through FF;
- The following status flags are used to determine the condition for branches:

> Negative
> Overflow
> Zero
> Carry

- The condition is true when the specified flag is set to one;
- The condition is false when the specified flat is reset to zero;
- Hexadecimal numbers can be interpreted as negative values if they are in the range of 80 through FF and as positive values when they are in the range of 1 through 7F;
- All branch instructions consider zero a positive value.

EXERCISES

1. When the following instruction is being executed, at what memory location is the Program Counter pointing?

_____

(1010, 1011, or 1012)

Memory	Op Code	Instruction
1010	D0	BNE
1011	F9	

2. What status flag will determine whether the branch in Exercise 1 is taken or not? _____ flag

3. Which direction (forward or backward) will the branch in Exercise 1 be taken? _____

4. Using the tables in Figures 6-1 and 6-2, give the hex operand that should be used to make the following branches:

   (a) forward 38 decimal steps _____
   (b) backward 100 decimal steps _____
   (c) forward 93 decimal steps _____
   (d) backward 42 decimal steps _____

5. Give the two-byte branch instruction which would branch backward 11 decimal steps if the result of an operation were positive.

Op Code	Mnemonic
_____	_____

_____

6. If two hex values are added and the result is greater than FF, what flag will be set?

_____

(Negative, Zero, or Carry)

7. What hex value would be in the accumulator following the execution of these two instructions? _____

     LDA #$7A
     ADC #$87

8. Tell the contents (0 or 1) of the following flags after the two instructions in Exercise 7 have been executed.

Zero flag _____
Negative flag _____
Carry flag _____

9. Tell which mode of the assembler is used for the following: (Modes are: EDIT, ASM, OR DEBUG)

  (a) to LIST a source program _____
  (b) to run an object program _____
  (c) to display a memory location used to store a result in a machine language program _____
  (d) to trace an object program _____

10. Tell what the following mnemonic codes represent:

  (a) BCC _____
  (b) BEQ _____
  (c) BPL _____
  (d) BCS _____
  (e) BNE _____
  (f) BMI _____

ANSWERS

1. 1012 (always one instruction ahead)
2. Zero flag
3. Backward
4. (a) 26
  (b) 9C
  (c) 5D
  (d) D6

5.   Op Code   Mnemonic
            10   BPL
            F5

6. Carry flag for sure (Possibly N,Z)

7. 01

8. Zero flag   0
   Negative flag 0
   Carry flag   1

9. (a) EDIT
   (b) DEBUG
   (c) DEBUG
   (d) DEBUG

10. (a) Branch on Carry Clear
    (b) Branch on result EQual zero
    (c) Branch on result PLus
    (d) Branch on Carry Set
    (e) Branch on result Not Equal zero
    (f) Branch on result MInus

Chapter 7

Assembler Review

This chapter summarizes what you have learned about the Atari Assembler and adds some new features that have not been discussed so far.

An assembly language program is made up of statements containing statement numbers, labels, Op code mnemonics, operands, and comments. The program, which is written in the **Writer/Editor** mode of the Assembler Cartridge, is called the *source* program. You assemble the source program in the Assemble mode. This produces a machine language program, called the object program. The assembler places this program in memory. The object program is then executed in the Debug mode to produce the desired result.

SOURCE PROGRAM FORMAT

The source program is made up of statements that begin with a line number and is terminated by pressing the RETURN key. Statements are broken up into the following *fields*, some of which are optional.

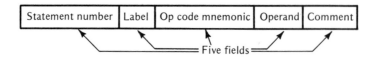

Figure 7-1. Statement Fields

Every statement must start with a statement number that is in the range of 0 through 65,535. You should number your statements in such a way that new ones may be inserted at a later time in case you want to alter your original program. Multiples of 10 work well for this purpose (i.e., 10,20,30,etc.). The Writer/Editor has convenient commands for automatically numbering or renumbering programs (see page 129). A statement may be up to 107 characters in length.

The label field is optional. If it is used, it follows the line number with *exactly one* space between the last digit of the line number and the first letter of the label. A label must start with a letter and contain only letters and numbers. It can be as short as two characters or as long as the limitation of the statement length. *If a label is not used*, two spaces or a tab is used between the statement number and the Op Code Mnemonic field (which follows the label field).

Examples:

With label

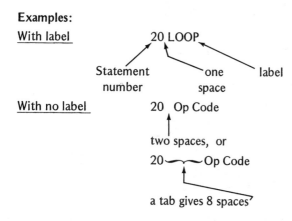

With no label

The Op Code Mnemonic must be one of those given in Appendix A or B. This field starts *at least* two spaces beyond the statement number (if no label is used) or *one space* after the label. A mnemonic placed in the wrong field will not be identified as an error in the Writer/Editor mode, but will be identified as Error –6 when you assemble the program (See Appendix D for Error codes.)

Examples:

With label

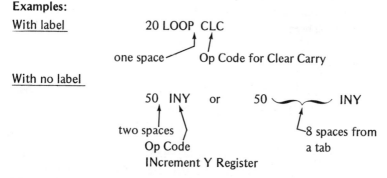

With no label

The field of the *operand* starts at least one space, or a tab, after the mnemonic field. Some Op Code mnemonics *require* an operand, while others do not. The form of the operand that is appropriate for each mnemonic code that uses one is given in Appendix A.

Examples:

<u>For hex operand</u>

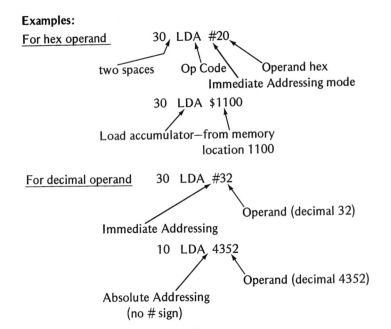

30 LDA #20

two spaces   Op Code   Operand hex
Immediate Addressing mode

30 LDA $1100

Load accumulator—from memory
location 1100

<u>For decimal operand</u>   30 LDA #32

Operand (decimal 32)

Immediate Addressing

10 LDA 4352

Operand (decimal 4352)

Absolute Addressing
(no # sign)

The last field, *comment*, appears on the listing of a source program but is not assembled. Therefore, it does not appear in the object program. There are two ways to enter comments.

- One way is to enter it in the comment field which occupies the remainder of the statement following the operand (if there is one) or the mnemonic code (if there is no operand). At least one space separates it from the last field used. There may not be enough room to put the entire comment in its field. In that case, you can extend your comment into the next line.

Examples:

20   CLC GET READY FOR ADDITION

comment

30   BNE LOOP IF THE COUNT HAS NOT   Extend comment
      REACHED ZERO GO BACK TO LOOP   to new line
                                           (no line number)

- A second way is to put the comment on its own line. In that case, one space follows the statement number, and a semicolon is used before the comment.

Examples:

30　CLC
40　;GET READY FOR ADDITION
　　　　　　　and
30　BNE LOOP IF THE COUNT HAS NOT
40　;REACHED ZERO GO BACK TO LOOP

METHODS TO USE OPERANDS

Line numbers, Op Code Mnemonics, and comments are straightforward and easy to use. The operands are sometimes tricky and deserve some more explanation.

Operands may be in the form of hexadecimal numbers, decimal numbers, or letters. The programmer has the option to use whichever form is desired.

A number used as an operand is interpreted as a decimal number by the assembler unless it is preceded by a $ sign. If a $ precedes the number, it is interpreted as a hexadecimal number.

Examples:

40　LDA 4500　　← 4500 is interpreted as a decimal number
50　STA $1100　　← $1100 is interpreted as a hexadecimal number

If a group of letters has been used as a label or have been assigned a numeric value, the letters may be used as an operand.

Examples:

20　ABC=$33
30　DEF=51
40　LOOP CLC
.
.
.　　　　　　　　　　　　LOOP was used as a label previously
.
80　BNE LOOP
90　CMP DEF
　　　or　　　　　　　　Decimal value 51
.
.
90　CMP $ABC　◄────Hexadecimal value 33

In addition to providing data, the operand also tells the computer what addressing mode to use for the operation specified by the Op Code Mnemonic.

Examples:

20	LDA #12	The # sign indicates the Immediate Addressing mode
30	CPY $1212	Absolute Addressing mode (no # sign)
40	STA $1250, Y	Absolute Indexed mode (note: ,Y added)
50	ADC ($2B,X)	Indexed Indirect mode (note: parentheses)
60	CMP ($3C),Y	Indirect Indexed mode (note: placement of parentheses)
70	INC $3C	Zero Page mode
80	INC $20,X	Indexed Zero Page mode

THE ASSEMBLER WRITER/EDITOR MODE

The Writer/Editor mode (referred to as the Edit mode for convenience) controls the communication between you, through the keyboard, and the video screen. When you power up your Atari with the Assembler Cartridge installed, you should see the Edit mode prompt on the screen. If you do not see the Edit prompt at this time, some error or malfunction has occurred. Check your Operator's Manual to make sure you have followed all procedures correctly.

Any entries from the keyboard will now appear in successive locations across the screen starting at the cursor ( ) position. The screen is 38 locations wide. If the end of a line is reached, there is an automatic "wrap around" so that your entries continue on the next line.

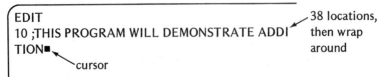

We have discussed some of the following commands used in the Edit mode. Others are new to you.

1. SIZE is used to find the location of the Current Line Buffer and Edit Text Buffer. Three numbers are displayed when the SIZE command is executed.

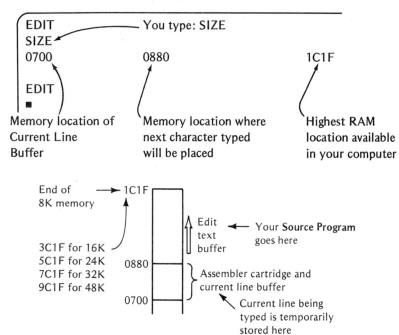

Memory location of Current Line Buffer

Memory location where next character typed will be placed

Highest RAM location available in your computer

Figure 7-2. Buffer Memory

The middle number in the example (0880) increases as the Edit Text Buffer is filled by your program. Therefore, the SIZE command can be used to find out how much memory is being used as you enter the **Source Program**. The machine language **Object Program** should be placed at memory locations higher than that occupied by your **Source Program**.

2. LOMEM is used to change the location of the Buffer Memory area. You have not used this command yet and may never use it. If you wanted to use 256 memory locations between 0700 and 0800 in your assembled program, you would use the LOMEM command like this:

```
EDIT
LOMEM 800

EDIT
■
```

Your memory would now be organized for use as shown in Figure 7-3.

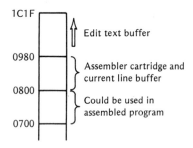

Figure 7-3. Altered Buffer Memory

Now give the SIZE command again.

```
EDIT
LOMEM 800

EDIT
SIZE
0800              0980              1C1F

EDIT
■
```

The location of the buffer areas cannot be changed after you have started writing a program. If you use the LOMEM command, *it must be the first command after you power up.*

3. LIST is used to display, on the video screen, the program that is currently in the Edit Text Buffer. It can be used in several forms.

(a) LIST to display the whole program

```
EDIT
LIST

10    *=$1000
20    CLC
30    LDA #0
40    LOOP ADC #1
50    CMP #$FF
60    BNE LOOP
70    END

EDIT
■
```

(b)　LIST 40 to display only line 40

```
EDIT
LIST 40

40   LOOP ADC #1

EDIT
■
```

(c)　LIST 50,70 to display all lines 50 through 70

```
EDIT
LIST 50,70

50      CMP #$FF
60      BNE LOOP
70      END

EDIT
■
```

4. NEW is used to clear the Edit Text Buffer. It does not clear the memory occupied by a previously assembled machine language program—only the Edit Text Buffer. After this command has been executed, you cannot restore any **Source Program** that existed previously in the Edit Text Buffer.

If the program in 3a under LIST is in the Edit Text Buffer, and you type NEW, the Edit Text Buffer will be cleared.

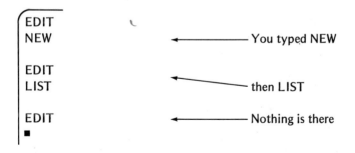

```
EDIT
NEW                  ◄─────────── You typed NEW

EDIT
LIST                 ◄─────────── then LIST

EDIT                 ◄─────────── Nothing is there
■
```

5. DEL is used to delete statements from the Edit Text Buffer. You have not used this command. It allows you to delete one line or several successive lines.

Suppose the program of 3a is still in the Edit Text Buffer, and you want to delete line 20.

```
EDIT
DEL 20

EDIT
LIST

10    *=$1000              ——— Line 20 is gone
30    LDA #0          ◄———
40    LOOP ADC #1
50    CMP #$FF
60    BNE LOOP
70   END

EDIT
■
```

Now, take out lines 40, 50, and 60.

```
EDIT
DEL 40,60

EDIT
LIST

10    *=$1000
30    LDA #0                  ← Not much left now
70   END

EDIT
■
```

6. REP is used to replace a specified string in the Edit Text Buffer with a different specified string. Thus, a program change can be quickly made by one of the several forms of this command. Suppose you once again have the program of 3a in the Edit Text Buffer.

(a) To replace the first occurrence of the string "LDA #0" with "LDA #5":

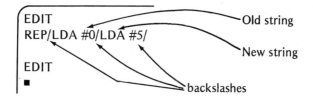

(b) To replace all occurrences of the string "LOOP" with the string "CIRCLE":

Lines 40 and 60 would be changed to:
```
40    CIRCLE ADC #1
50    BNE CIRCLE
```
Other forms of this command are explained in the Atari Assembler Manual.

7. NUM is used to number the statements automatically in an assembly language program. It can be used in several forms.

(a) To increment the statement numbers by 10:

```
 EDIT
 NUM

 10 ■          ← Prints a 10 and skips one space
```

Type in the first line and press RETURN

```
 EDIT
 NUM

 10  *=$1000   ← Type another space, *=$1000 and
 20  ■             press RETURN

            Prints 20 and skips one space
```

(b) To increment by a value different than 10:

```
EDIT
NUM 3

3                ◄── Now starts at 3
```
Type in first line and press RETURN

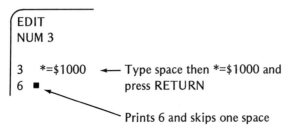

```
EDIT
NUM 3

3    *=$1000   ◄── Type space then *=$1000 and
6 ■                press RETURN
```
Prints 6 and skips one space

(c) To force a new line and change the increment (or the starting line):

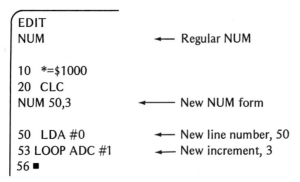

```
EDIT
NUM             ◄── Regular NUM

10  *=$1000
20  CLC
NUM 50,3        ◄──── New NUM form

50  LDA #0      ◄── New line number, 50
53 LOOP ADC #1  ◄── New increment, 3
56 ■
```

Press RETURN to cancel the NUM command.

```
 .
 .
50  LDA #0
53 LOOP ADC #1
56              Press RETURN here
 ■              NUM is no longer active
```

8. REN is used to renumber statements in the Edit Text Buffer.

(a) To renumber statements in increments of 10 starting with 10, type:
REN   then press RETURN

(b) To renumber statements in increments of 5 starting with line number 10, type:
REN 5   and press RETURN

(c) To renumber all statements in increments of 2 starting with line number 20, type:

REN 20,2   and press RETURN

9. ASM is used to transfer from the **Writer/Editor Program** to the **Assembler Program.**

10. BUG is used to transfer from the **Writer/Editor Program** to the **Debug Program.**

There are also commands to save and retrieve programs or specific blocks of memory. Their use is described in the Atari Assembler Manual and will not be repeated here. Each of these commands

LIST, ENTER, ASM, SAVE, and LOAD

are used in several forms depending on whether you wish to use the video screen, printer, cassette recorder, or disk drive.

THE DEBUG MODE

The Debug mode, which is entered from the Writer/Editor mode by typing "BUG", allows you to alter or execute the **Object Program** that has been assembled. It also allows you to enter and change data tables that the **Object Program** uses. The prompt shown on the video display when you are in this mode is the word, DEBUG.

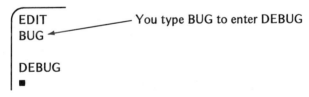

```
EDIT                 ——— You type BUG to enter DEBUG
BUG

DEBUG
■
```

The command to return to the Writer/Editor mode from the Debug mode is the letter, X.

```
EDIT
BUG                 ← Type BUG to enter Debug mode

DEBUG
X                   ← Type X to leave Debug

EDIT                ← Now you're back in the
■                     Writer/Editor mode
```

To demonstrate the commands used in the Debug mode, enter the following program.

```
EDIT
NUM              ◄── For automatic numbering by 10

10    *=$1000
20    LDY #0
30    LDA #0
40   LOOP CLC
50    INY
60    ADC #1
70    CPY #3
80    BNE LOOP
90   END
100 ■
```

Now assemble the program.

```
.
.
.
.
80    BNE LOOP
90   END

ASM■              Type: ASM and press RETURN
```

0000	10	*=	$1000
1000 A000	20	LDY	#0
1002 A900	30	LDA	#0
1004 18	40 LOOP	CLC	
1005 C8	50	INY	
1006 6901	60	ADC #1	
1008 C003	70	CPY #3	
100A D0F8	80	BNE LOOP	
	90 END		
EDIT			
■			

Now, go to the Debug mode.

EDIT
BUG

DEBUG
■

There are three ways to execute a program. The method that you choose will depend on whether you want to display the steps as they are executed or not.

1. To execute the program without a display, type: G1000 and press the RETURN key.

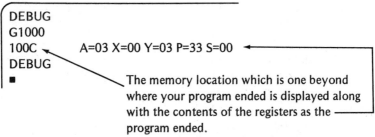

DEBUG
G1000
100C   A=03 X=00 Y=03 P=33 S=00
DEBUG
■

The memory location which is one beyond where your program ended is displayed along with the contents of the registers as the program ended.

Register A (the accumulator) contains a 3. The Y register also contains a 3. This is as you would expect.

2. To TRACE a program, type T1000 and press RETURN. The display will show each instruction as it is executed along with the contents of the registers after the instruction has been executed.

```
DEBUG
T1000
1000        A0 00            LDY     #$00
    A=00 X=00 Y=00 P=33 S=00
1002        A9 00            LDA     #$00
    A=00 X=00 Y=00 P=33 S=00
1004        18               CLC
    A=00 X=00 Y=00 P=32 S=00
1005        C8               INY
    A=00 X=00 Y=01 P=32 S=00
        :
    etc., until the program has ended
```

3. To SINGLE STEP through a program, type S1000 and press RETURN. The display will show the results of the first instruction. To continue the single step procedure, type the letter S and press the RETURN key for each successive instruction that you want executed.

```
DEBUG
S1000
1000        A0 00              LDY    #$00
    A=03 X=00 Y=00 P=33 S=00
DEBUG
S
1002        A9 00              LDA    #$00
    A=00 X=00 Y=00 P=33 S=00
DEBUG
S
1004        18                 CLC
    A=00 X=00 Y=00 P=32 S=00
DEBUG
■
```

4. To DISPLAY the contents of memory, type the letter D followed by the address of the memory location that you want to examine.

(a) To display a single memory location.

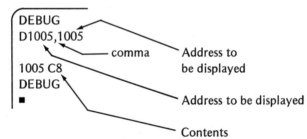

```
DEBUG
D1005,1005
                    — comma      Address to
1005 C8                          be displayed
DEBUG
■
```

Address to be displayed

Contents

(b) To display up to 8 consecutive locations

```
DEBUG               — Only the starting
D1000                 address is given

1000    A0 00 A9 00 18 C8 69 01
DEBUG
■
```

(c) To display more than 8 consecutive locations, type D, the starting address, a comma, and the ending address.

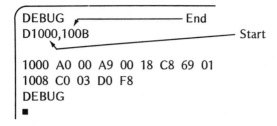

```
DEBUG ┌────────────── End
D1000,100B ──────────────── Start

1000 A0 00 A9 00 18 C8 69 01
1008 C0 03 D0 F8
DEBUG
■
```

(d) Notice that in b and c above, memory was displayed with a block of 8 locations per full line. This will result when the requested starting location ends in 0 or 8 (i.e., 1000, 1008, 1010, 1018, etc.) However, if the starting address does not end in 0 or 8, a block containing fewer than 8 values will be displayed on the first line.

Examples:

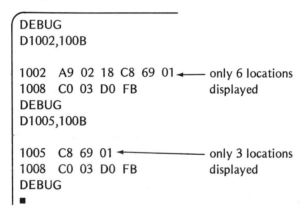

```
DEBUG
D1002,100B

1002  A9 02 18 C8 69 01 ◄──── only 6 locations
1008  C0 03 D0 FB            displayed
DEBUG
D1005,100B

1005  C8 69 01 ◄──────────── only 3 locations
1008  C0 03 D0 FB            displayed
DEBUG
■
```

5. You can LIST a block of memory with the contents DISASSEMBLED into assembly language mnemonics. Type L followed by the starting address or the starting and ending address, just as you do for the display command.

(a) For only one instruction:

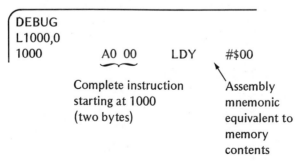

```
DEBUG
L1000,0
1000          A0 00      LDY     #$00
```

                     Complete instruction   Assembly
                     starting at 1000   mnemonic
                     (two bytes)   equivalent to
                                                    memory
                                                contents

```
.
.
DEBUG
L1004,0
1004                18          CLC
```
Complete instructions ← → Assembly
starting at 1004   mnemonic
(one byte)

(b) For several instructions:

```
.
.
.
DEBUG
L1000,1005
1000        A0 00       LDY   #$00
1002        A9 00       LDA   #$00
1004        18          CLC
1005        C8          INY

DEBUG
■
```

(c) Since the DEBUGGER starts disassembling from the specified start-
     ing location, you must be sure that the specified starting location
     corresponds to the first byte of some instruction in your program.
     Otherwise the DEBUGGER is confused, or interprets the code as
     something different than intended.

     (1) Confusion:

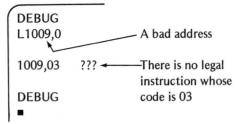

```
DEBUG
L1009,0                    ——— A bad address

1009,03    ??? ←——————There is no legal
                            instruction whose
DEBUG                       code is 03
■
```

     (2) Misleading address:

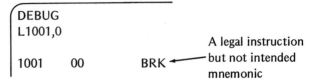

```
DEBUG
L1001,0
                              A legal instruction
1001    00          BRK ←——— but not intended
                              mnemonic
```

6. As shown in earlier programs, the contents of memory can be changed.

(a) Changing one address:

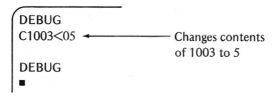

```
DEBUG
C1003<05  ─────────────── Changes contents
                          of 1003 to 5
DEBUG
■
```

(b) Changing successive locations. The comma increments the location to be changed.

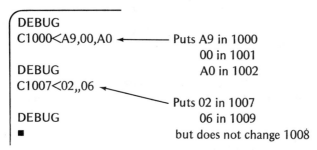

```
DEBUG
C1000<A9,00,A0  ─────── Puts A9 in 1000
                        00 in 1001
DEBUG                   A0 in 1002
C1007<02,,06
                ─────── Puts 02 in 1007
DEBUG                   06 in 1009
■                       but does not change 1008
```

7. The contents of a block of memory can be MOVED to a different memory area.

Example:

Original Memory Location	Memory Contents
1100	40
1101	41
1102	42
1103	43

The move command is then given.

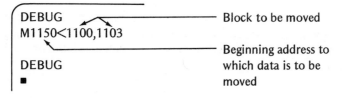

```
DEBUG             ─────────────── Block to be moved
M1150<1100,1103

                  ─────────────── Beginning address to
DEBUG                              which data is to be
■                                  moved
```

Memory now looks like this:

Memory Location	Memory Contents
1100	40
1101	41
1102	42
1103	43
.	.
.	.
.	.
1150	40
1151	41
1152	42
1153	43

This data copied ─────────

8. To VERIFY that data has been moved as desired or that two blocks of memory contain the same data, you can compare two blocks of memory.

Example:

Using the results of item 7.

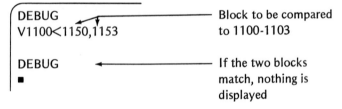

DEBUG
V1100<1150,1153 ─────── Block to be compared to 1100-1103

DEBUG
■ ◄─────── If the two blocks match, nothing is displayed

If 1151 contains 31, not 41:

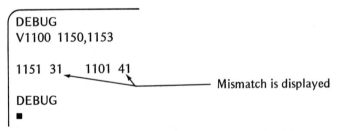

DEBUG
V1100 1150,1153

1151 31   1101 41 ─────── Mismatch is displayed
DEBUG
■

Other commands and variations of the ones shown in this chapter are given in the Atari Assembler Manual. You should explore the manual thoroughly and experiment with all commands so that you can use all the facilities of the Assembler Cartridge.

Since this entire chapter is a summary of the Assembler commands, no chapter summary is given. Go right on to the chapter exercises.

EXERCISES

1. The five statement fields of a **Source Program** are given below. Tell which are always used and which are somtimes used in a **Source Program** statement.

    (a) Statement number _____

    (b) Label _____

    (c) Op Code Mnemonic _____

    (d) Operand _____

    (e) Comment _____

2. The assembler will interpret some numbers as decimal and others as hexadecimal depending on the specified operand. Give the interpretation of the following:

    (a) LDA #$13 _____

    (b) LDY #14 _____

3. The SIZE command is given, and the computer displays:

```
EDIT
SIZE
0700            0880            3C1F

EDIT
■
```

The computer is then turned off. It is then turned on and the following commands are given. Fill in the display as shown after the final SIZE command.

```
EDIT
LOMEM 900

EDIT
SIZE
_____    _____    _____

EDIT
■
```

Exercises 4 through 10 refer to the following program:

```
EDIT
LIST

10    *=$1000
20    CLC
30    LDA #0
40  LOOP ADC #5
50    CMP #$50
60    BNE LOOP
70  END
■
```

4. Give the value in the accumulator at the end of each of the first five passes through the loop.

   1st _____   4th _____
   2nd _____   5th _____
   3rd _____

5. (a) Will the accumulator ever contain the hexadecimal value 50?_____

   (b) If so, how many times will the loop be executed? _____

6. What would be the command used to list all lines from 30 through 60, inclusive? _____

7. Give the command that would delete line 20. _____

8. Give one command that will change the word LOOP in lines 40 and 60 to the word ROUND. _____

9. Give a command that would renumber the program starting with statement number 100 and numbering each successive statement in increments of 5.

_____

10. Give the command to enter the Debugger mode and show the prompt that results.

```
EDIT

_____

_____

■
```

The following exercises assume that the program preceding Exercise 4 has been assembled, and that you are now in the Debugger mode. The assembled **Object Program** is now stored in the following memory locations.

Memory	Contents
1000	18
1001	A9
1002	00
1003	69
1004	05
1005	C9
1006	50
1007	D0
1008	FA
1009	00

11. What is the command to:

   (a) execute the program _____

   (b) trace the program _____

   (c) single step the first instruction _____

12. If the command: D1000 is executed, show the displayed result.

```
DEBUG
D1000


DEBUG
■
```

13. Show the display resulting from the command: L1000,0

```
DEBUG
L1000,0


DEBUG
■
```

14. If you wanted to change the program so that it would add ten (hex 0A) each time through the loop instead of 5, show how to change one memory location to accomplish the change.

> DEBUG
>
> _____
>
> DEBUG
> ■

15. Show a command to move the program so that the first instruction will be in memory location 1120.

> DEBUG
>
> _____
>
> DEBUG
> ■

ANSWERS

1. (a) Always
   (b) Sometimes
   (c) Always
   (d) Sometimes (Some Op Codes require operands)
   (e) Sometimes

2. (a) Hexadecimal
   (b) Decimal

3.
> .
> .
> SIZE
> 0900   0A80   3C1F

4. 1st 05   4th 14
   2nd 0A   5th 19
   3rd 0F

5. (a) Yes
   (b) Sixteen times

6. LIST 30,50

7. DEL 20

8. REP/LOOP/ROUND/ ,A

9. REN 100,5

10.
```
EDIT
BUG

DEBUG
■
```

11. (a) G1000
    (b) T1000
    (c) S1000

12.
```
DEBUG
D1000
1000 18 A9 00 69 05 C9 50 D0

DEBUG
■
```

13.
```
DEBUG
L1000,0

1000            18            CLC

DEBUG
■
```

14.
```
DEBUG
C1004<0A

DEBUG
■
```

15.
```
DEBUG
M1120<1000,1009

DEBUG
■
```

Chapter 8

Designing a Program

A program is usually written to solve a specific problem. The method of solving the problem should be determined *before* any attempt is made to write the program to solve it. Since assembly language programming is not interactive like BASIC, a detailed plan is needed for each assembler program.

> Sample Problem: Add five pairs of two-digit
> numbers and store the results.

1. In analyzing the stated problem, you can see that some area of memory is needed to hold the five pairs of numbers that are to be added. These will be referred to as data tables.

2. You must also provide for five results. Since you will be *adding* two-digit numbers, the sum may be greater than two digits. Therefore, it will be necessary to provide for two memory locations for each sum. This group of memory locations will be called the result table.

3. The addition will be performed on two pairs of numbers at a time with the data being accessed from the data tables and the results stored in a different table.

4. You must allocate the necessary memory locations for the program as well as the data and result tables.

> NOTICE that you do not know at this time how long the assembled assembled program will be. Therefore, you must estimate where the starting location of the data will be. We allowed lots of room for the program.

Now that you have stated the problem in realistic terms, you should think through the program in functional blocks.

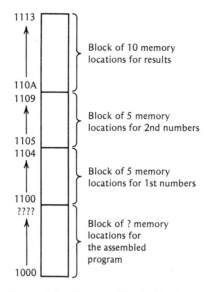

1113
110A
1109
1105
1104
1100
????
1000

Block of 10 memory
locations for results

Block of 5 memory
locations for 2nd numbers

Block of 5 memory
locations for 1st numbers

Block of ? memory
locations for
the assembled
program

Figure 8-1. Memory Blocks Used

A. | LOAD the data
    | into memory

B. | ADD the data and
    | STORE the results
    | in memory

Figure 8-2. Functional Blocks

Think about Block A. You could load the data into the correct memory locations using the Assembler Cartridge in the Debug mode. You could also load the data tables from the program itself. The latter method consumes time and memory space, so we will use the first method. It is more direct, is easily changed (if needed), keeps the program simple, and will enable you to use another Assembler Cartridge capability. Therefore, your program will be reduced to Block B.

Let's now expand Block B into functional parts.

Block B | 1. Load one 2-digit number
         | into the accumulator.
         | 2. Add the second 2-digit
         | number.
         | 3. Store the result.
         | 4. Go back and repeat until
         | all 5 sums are performed.

Figure 8-3. Block B Parts

The Absolute Indexed Addressing mode will be the most efficient way to load, add and store the numbers. You can use both X and Y registers to index the instructions. The program might consist of the following.

ADD FIVE PAIRS OF NUMBERS

	LDY	#0	Load the Y register with an initial value of zero. This will index the load and add instructions as well as serving as a loop counter.
	LDX	#0	Load the X register with a value of zero. X will serve to index the pair of stored results.
LOOP	CLC		Start of loop. Clear Carry bit in preparation for adding a pair of numbers.
	LDA	$1100,Y	Load the accumulator from memory location 1100+Y.
	ADC	$1105,Y	Add with carry the number in memory location 1105+Y.
	STA	$110B,X	Store the least significant byte of sum in memory location 110B+X.
	BCC	SKIP	If there was no carry, branch to the instruction labeled SKIP.
	INC	$110A,X	If there was a carry, increment memory location 110A+X.
SKIP	INX		Increase X by two for
	INX		two-byte result
	INY		Increase Y by one for next load and sum.
	CPY	#5	See if Y = 5
	BNE	LOOP	If Y ≠ 5, branch back to instruction labeled LOOP for next pair of numbers.
END			End of the program

ABSOLUTE INDEXED ADDRESSING

The load, add, increment, and store instructions are all used in the Absolute Indexed Addressing mode. In this mode, a base address is specified. The value contained in either the X or Y register is added to the base address to obtain the memory address actually used.

Examples:

Suppose the Y register holds the value 3, the X register holds 6, and the following values are in memory.

Memory	Value
1100	12
1101	34
1102	56
1103	78
1104	9A
1105	BC
1106	DE
1107	F0
1108	01
1109	23

Here is what happens when you execute the following instructions.

LDA $1100,Y   would load the accumulator from memory location 1100+3, or 1103

ACCUMULATOR   78

ADC $1105,Y   would add the value 78 to the value in memory location 1105+ 3, or 1108 (value is 01)

ACCUMULATOR   79

STA $110B,X   would store the value in the accumulator into memory location 110B+6, or 1111

MEMORY 1111   79

The value for X and Y is originally loaded as zero. The Y value is incremented once each time through the loop, and the X register is incremented twice each time. Thus, a new value is loaded, a new value is added, and the result is stored in a new pair of locations.

Y=	X=	Loaded value from	Added value from	Result stored in
0	0	1100	1105	110A and 110B
1	2	1101	1106	110C and 110D
2	4	1102	1107	110E and 110F
3	6	1103	1108	1110 and 1111
4	8	1104	1109	1112 and 1113
5	A	END OF PROGRAM		

Figure 8-4. How Memory is Used

Now you are ready to use the computer with the Assembler Cartridge.

USING THE ADD FIVE PAIRS OF NUMBERS PROGRAM

With the Assembler Cartridge in the left slot of the Atari, you might first input the program from the Edit mode.

```
EDIT
10      *=$1000
20      LDY #0
30      LDX #0
40      LOOP CLC
50      LDA $1100,Y
60      ADC $1105,Y
70      STA $110B,X
80      BCC SKIP
90      INC $110A,X
100     SKIP INX
110     INX
120     INY
130     CPY #5
140     BNE LOOP
150     END
■
```

You then assemble the program.

```
150 END
ASM
0000            10      *=      $1000

1000  A000      20      LDY     $0

1002  A200      30      LDX     #0

1004  18        40 LOOP CLC

1005  B90011    50      LDA     $1100,Y

1008  790511    60      ADC     $1105,Y
```

100B	9D0B11	70	STA	$110B,X
100E	9003	80	BCC	SKIP
1010	FE0A11	90	INC	$110A,X
1013	E8	100 SKIP	INX	
1014	E8	110	INX	
1015	C8	120	INY	
1016	C005	130	CPY #5	
1018	D0EA	140	BNE LOOP	
		150 END		

EDIT
■

Next, you must place the data in the appropriate tables. Notice that you are putting zeros in the result table. This must be done to make sure the locations used for the high-order bytes of the result are filled with zeros originally. Since you are using the INCrement instruction to place the carry bit into the high-order byte of the result, you must make sure that a zero is in the memory to begin with. You must be in the Debug mode to enter the data.

```
.
.
140    BNE LOOP
150    END
BUG

DEBUG
■
```

The DEBUG Command for changing values in memory is:

CXXXX<yy   where the X's represent hexadecimal digits in the memory address to be changed. The y's represent the one- or two-digit hex number to be placed in the specified memory location.

To change a number of consecutive memory locations the command takes the following form.

CXXXX<aa,bb,cc,dd   where XXXX is the first memory location to be changed. aa,bb,etc., represent hex values to be inserted into consecutive memory locations starting at XXXX. Up to 16 data values may be inserted at one time. Then a new starting address is needed.

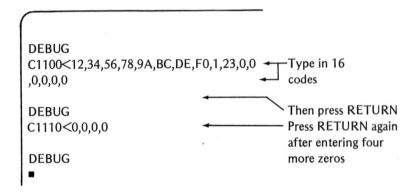

There, the data is all in place, and the program has been assembled. As one final check, use the DISPLAY Command in the Debug mode to look at the program and the data.

Display the program.

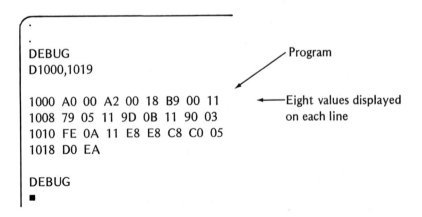

Check the hex codes against those on page 148. If they agree, then check the data.

```
.
.
.
DEBUG                                              data tables
D1100,1113

1100 12 34 56 78 9A BC DE F0
1108 01 23 00 00 00 00 00 00
1100 00 00 00 00

DEBUG
■
```

OK, now you can run the program.

```
.
.
.
DEBUG
G1000
101A           A=BD X=0A Y=05 P=33 S=00
DEBUG
■
```

Finally, check the results by displaying the result table.

```
.
.
.
DEBUG
D110A,110B

110A 00 CE     ←     12+BC = 00CE
DEBUG
D110C,110D

110C 01 12     ←     34+DE = 0112
DEBUG
D110E,110F

110E 01 46     ←     56+F0 = 0146
DEBUG
D1110,1111

1110 00 79     ←     78+01 = 0079
DEBUG
D1112,1113

1112 00 BD     ←     9A+23 = BD
DEBUG
■
```

Suppose the sample problem changes. Instead of adding the ten numbers in pairs, you might want to add all ten numbers together.

Sample Problem 2: Add ten two-digit numbers and store the result.

Once again, expand Block B of the Functional Blocks of Figure 8-2. This time we want to:

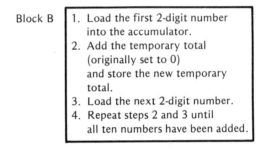

Block B
1. Load the first 2-digit number into the accumulator.
2. Add the temporary total (originally set to 0) and store the new temporary total.
3. Load the next 2-digit number.
4. Repeat steps 2 and 3 until all ten numbers have been added.

*Figure 8-5. Block B Parts—***Add Ten Program**

Notice the differences between the solutions to Sample Problem 1 and Sample Problem 2.

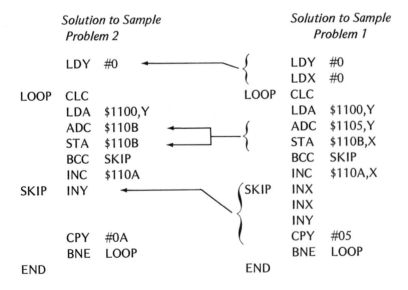

Solution to Sample			*Solution to Sample*	
Problem 2			*Problem 1*	
	LDY	#0	LDY	#0
			LDX	#0
LOOP	CLC		LOOP	CLC
	LDA	$1100,Y		LDA	$1100,Y
	ADC	$110B		ADC	$1105,Y
	STA	$110B		STA	$110B,X
	BCC	SKIP		BCC	SKIP
	INC	$110A		INC	$110A,X
SKIP	INY		SKIP	INX
				INX
				INY
	CPY	#0A		CPY	#05
	BNE	LOOP		BNE	LOOP
END			END	

You can see that the solution to Sample Problem 2 uses fewer instructions than the solution to Sample Problem 1. The temporary and final sum is stored in memory locations 110A and 110B. The temporary sum is added to each two-digit number each time the loop is executed, and the new sum is stored back in the same location. For that reason, the X register is not needed in the second solution.

This is how the memory locations are used as each two-digit number is added.

Loop Number	Accumulator Loaded	Temporary Sum	110A 110B Stored	
1	12	00+12	00	12
2	34	12+34	00	46
3	56	46+56	00	9C
4	78	9C+78	01	14
5	9A	14+9A	01	AE
6	BC	AE+BC	02	6A
.	.	.	.	.
.	.	.	.	.
.	.	.	.	.

etc.

Figure 8-6. Memory Use in **Add Ten Program**

USING THE ADD TEN PROGRAM

The steps to use the program follow previous directions. We will not give the steps in detail, but we will show the results.

In the Edit mode:

1. Enter the Program.

2. Assemble the Program.

In the Debug mode:

3. Load the data.

4. Run the program.

5. Display results.

1. Enter the Program.

```
10      *=$1000
20      LDY #0
30      LOOP CLC
40      LDA $1100,Y
50      ADC $110B
60      STA $110B
70      BCC SKIP
80      INC $110A
90      SKIP INY
100     CPY #10
110     BNE LOOP
120     END
```

Note that we can enter the
number of steps (10) as:
    #10 for decimal values
        or
    #$10 for hexadecimal values

This indicates hex.

2. Assemble the program.

```
ASM

0000              10      *=      $1000

1000  A000        20      LDY  #0

1002  18          30 LOOP  CLC

1003  B90011      40      LDA  $1100,Y

1006  6D0B11      50      ADC  $110B

1009  8D0B11      60      STA  $110B

100C  9003        70      BCC  SKIP

100E  EE0A11      80      INC  $110A

1011  C8          90 SKIP  INY                    #10 in decimal

1012  C00A        0100    CPY  #10                Assembled as a
                                                  hex value, OA
1014  D0EC        0110    BNE  LOOP

                  0120 END
```

3. Load the data in the Debug mode.

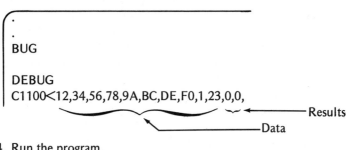

```
.
.
BUG

DEBUG
C1100<12,34,56,78,9A,BC,DE,F0,1,23,0,0,
```
                                                  ——Results
                                      ——Data

4. Run the program.

```
DEBUG
G1000
1016          A=5C X=00 Y=0A P=33 S=00
```

5. Display the result.

```
DEBUG
D110A,110B
110A  04  5C  ◄—— Result in locations 110A and 110B
```

A VARIATION OF THE ADD TEN PROGRAM

There is usually more than one way to program a solution to a problem, and a good programmer is continually seeking ways to make his programs more efficient. Let's look at a slight variation of the last program that eliminates one two-byte instruction.

THE TWO ADD TEN PROGRAMS

First Program				Second Program		
10	*=$1000			10	*=$1000	
20	LDY	#0	◄——***——►	20	LDY	#10
30	LOOP	CLC		30	LOOP	CLC
40	LDA	$1100,Y		40	LDA	$1100,Y
50	ADC	$110B		50	ADC	$110C
60	STA	$110B		60	STA	$110C
70	BCC	SKIP		70	BCC	SKIP
80	INC	$110A		80	INC	$110B
90	SKIP	INY	◄——***——►	90	SKIP	DEY
100	CPY	#10	◄——***—┐	100	BNE	LOOP
110	BNE	LOOP	omitted ┘	110	END	
120	END					

*** denotes program changes

The second program counts downward from ten to zero as the loop is executed over and over. Because of this, the results and data tables are placed in slightly different memory locations. Each value is offset by one location.

One instruction, CPY #10, is omitted from the second program. This is possible because the zero bit of the Processor Status Register is set when the Y register is decremented to zero after the last time through the loop. Therefore, the BNE instruction can be used directly following the DEY instruction with no comparison necessary. Since you were counting upwards from 0 through 10 in the first program, the value in the Y register had to be compared to ten before the BNE instruction could be used.

A comparison of the assembled programs shows that the second program is two bytes shorter. It ends at memory location 1013, whereas the first program ended at memory location 1015.

The data tables are accessed similarly for the two programs, but the memory addresses are offset in the second program due to the way that the Y register is decremented.

First Program

0000		10	*=	$1000
1000	A000	20	LDY	#0
1002	18	30 LOOP	CLC	
1003	B90011	40	LDA	$1100,Y
1006	6D0B11	50	ADC	$110B
1009	8D0B11	60	STA	$110B
100C	9003	70	BCC	SKIP
100E	EE0A11	80	INC	$110A
1011	C8	90 SKIP	INY	
1012	C00A	0100	CPY	#10 ←—————— this instruction unnecessary in
1014	D0ED	0110	BNE	LOOP second program
		0120 END		

Second Program

0000		10	*=	$1000	
1000	A00A	20	LDY	#10	← initial value 10 instead of zero
1002	18	30 LOOP	CLC		
1003	B90011	40	LDA	$1100,Y	
1006	6D0C11	50	ADC	$110C	different memory
1009	8D0C11	60	STA	$110C	locations used
100C	9003	70	BCC	SKIP	
100E	EE0B11	80	INC	$110B	
1011	88	90 SKIP	DEY		← counting down
1012	D0EE	0100	BNE LOOP		
		0110 END			

	First Program Tables			Second Program Tables	
	Data	Memory	Data		
	12	1100	Not used		↑
	34	1101	12		
	56	1102	34		
Data	78	1103	56		
accessed	9A	1104	78		Data
in this	BC	1105	9A		accessed
order	DE	1106	BC		in reverse
	F0	1107	DE		order
	01	1108	F0		
↓	23	1109	01		
	Low-byte result	110A	23		
	High-byte result	110B	Low-byte result		
	Not used	110C	High-byte result		

Figure 8-7. Data Tables

Naturally, executing the second program produces the same result as the first even though the numbers are added in the reverse order.

One new instruction was introduced in the second program.

DEY (DEcrement the Y register)
Op Code 88

It is a one-byte instruction used only in the Implied Addressing mode. It works just the opposite as INY (Increment Y). The value in the Y register is decreased (or decremented) by one when the instruction is executed.

Some programmers might object to the changes in the locations of the data tables. This change was done so that the branch instruction could make direct use of the condition of the zero bit following the DEY instruction. If the data was located as in the first program, the following sequence would result on the last pass through the loop.

Old Y	Instruction Executed	Present Sum	Memory Last Accessed	New Y
1	SKIP DEY	04 4A	1101	0
0	BNE LOOP	04 4A		

Sets zero bit in
Processor Status
Register

Since the zero bit is set, the branch would not be taken back for the last number. Therefore, the final sum (044A) would be incorrect.

YET ANOTHER VARIATION

Another variation could be used to keep the data tables in their original position, but it would require that you change the order of the instructions and move the CPY instruction back into the program.

Third Program

```
10       *=$1000
20       LDY   #10
30       LOOP   DEY   ◄———— Move DEY up here
40       CLC
50       LDA   $1100,Y ◄——— For Y values of 9,8,7,
60       ADC   $110B              6,5,4,3,2,1,0
70       STA   $110B
80       BCC   SKIP
90       INC   $110A ◄——— Back to original values
100      SKIP  CPY #0
110      BNE   LOOP         CPY back in
120      END
```

You can see that you have a considerable amount of freedom in designing a program. Any program is a *good program* if it solves the problem for which it was designed. Usually, good programs can be improved for efficiency and quickness of execution. Programming provides for large amounts of individualism and creativity. Enjoy it!

SUMMARY

- In this chapter you've learned how to design an assembly language program to solve a specific problem. The suggested steps are:

  1. Analyze the problem by deciding how the solution will be accomplished generally.
  2. Decide what memory locations will be used for data and results.
  3. Think through your solution in functional blocks.
  4. Expand each block into steps that the computer can handle.
  5. Write the program in terms of the expanded functional blocks.

- You learned how to handle data with tables accessed by the Absolute Indexed Addressing mode to load, add, and store data. Instructions used in this mode were:

  1. LDA $1100,Y   Load data into the accumulator from memory (location 1100+the value in the Y register)
  2. ADC $1105,Y   Add the data from memory (location 1105+the value of Y register) to the data in the accumulator

3. STA $110B,X   Store the accumulator's contents into memory (location 110B+the value in the X register)

4. INC $110A,X   Increment the content of memory (location 110A+ the value in the X register)

- You learned to enter data with the change memory command in the Debug mode.

Examples:

C1100<12,34,56,78,9A,BC,DE,F0,1,23,0,0

,0,0,0,0

16 items entered consecutively starting at memory location 1100

C1110<0,0,0,0

4 more items entered consecutively starting at memory location 1110

- You learned that an index register can count down as well as up.

Down →   DEY Decrement the Y register

Up →   INY Increment the Y register

- You learned to change a program to solve a new problem and to make variations of existing programs.

- You learned that there may be several ways to program a solution to a given problem.

EXERCISES

1. In which mode (EDIT, ASM, or DEBUG) were the data entries loaded into memory for the programs in this chapter? _____

2. What addressing mode is used for the following instruction?

   STA $1500,Y

   _____

3. If the accumulator holds a value of 10, and the Y register holds 5, into what memory location will the 10 be stored if the instruction in Exercise 2 is executed? _____

4. The following values are in the computer as shown.

Accumulator	Memory	Data	Y Register
12	1100	D5	1
	1101	33	
	1102	22	
	1103	24	

Then the following sequence of instructions is executed. Fill in the data in the appropriate blanks below.

LDA $1100,Y
ADC $1101,Y
INY
STA $1100,Y

Accumulator	Memory	Data	Y Register
	1100		
	1101		
	1102		
	1103		

5. If the instructions of Exercise 4 were executed again using your results for Exercise 4, what would the new values be?

Accumulator	Memory	Data	Y Register
	1100		
	1101		
	1102		
	1103		

6. Suppose you are in the Debug mode, and you execute the command:

C1100<A4,F3,C5,19

Show what would be in the following memory locations.

Memory	Data
1100	
1101	
1102	
1103	
1104	

Hint: One of the memory locations is not changed by the command. Place an XX in that location.

7. Give one DEBUG command to display all four memory locations of Exercise
5. _____

8. Fill in the blanks in the table below for the following program.

```
10      *=$1000
20      LDY #0
30      LOOP CLC
40      LDA $1101,Y
50      ADC $1100,Y
60      INY
70      STA $1100,Y
80      CPY #4
90      BNE LOOP
100     END
```

End of	Y	Accumulator	Memory				
Loop	Register		1100	1101	1102	1103	1104
0	0	00	01	02	03	04	05
1							
2							
3							
4							

9. Show the hex and decimal values for the following Assembler notations.

#24 _____ hex = _____ decimal
#$24_____ hex = _____ decimal

ANSWERS

1. DEBUG

2. Absolute Indexed Addressing

3. 1505 (hex)

4.
Accumulator		Memory	Data	Y Register

Accumulator

55

Memory	Data
1101	D5
1101	33
1102	55
1103	24

Y Register

2

5.   Accumulator

| 79 |

Memory	Data
1100	D5
1101	33
1102	55
1103	79

Y Register

| 3 |

6.

Memory	Data
1100	A4
1101	F3
1102	C5
1103	19
1104	XX

← (don't know)

7. D1100,1103

8.

At End of loop #	Y Register	Accumulator	Memory				
			1100	1101	1102	1103	1104
0	0	00	01	02	03	04	05
1	1	03	01	03	03	04	05
2	2	06	01	03	06	04	05
3	3	0A	01	03	06	0A	05
4	4	0F	01	03	06	0A	0F

9. #24   18 hex = 24 decimal
   #$24   24 hex = 36 decimal

Chapter 9

Addition and Subtraction

You are now familiar with the way that computers add and subtract numbers. Since the size of registers and memory is limited to 8 binary digits, addition and subtraction must be performed with pieces of data of the same size. Keep in mind that the largest decimal integer that can be expressed in 8 bits (one byte) is 255.

You learned in Chapter 6 to test for the Carry bit to see if the sum of two 8-bit numbers was larger than the accumulator could hold.

Example:

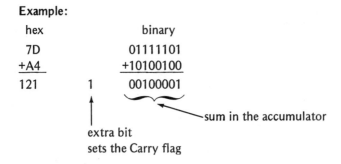

```
hex                 binary
 7D               01111101
+A4              +10100100
121        1      00100001
```

sum in the accumulator

extra bit
sets the Carry flag

In this way you can tell when the sum of two 8-bit numbers is larger than can be held in a register or memory location. However at some time you will want to add numbers that are larger than 255. To accomplish this, the computer must handle the number in more than one byte. The computer can add a byte from each of two numbers, store the result, and then add the second bytes of the two numbers. Then you can display the two parts as one complete number.

Example:

hex	binary
6E61	0110111001100001
+219C	+0010000110011100
8FFD	

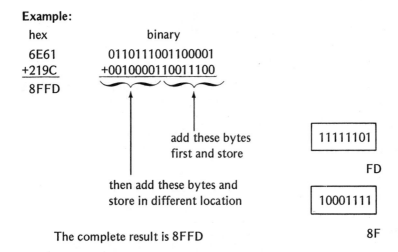

add these bytes
first and store

11111101

FD

then add these bytes and
store in different location

10001111

The complete result is 8FFD

8F

TWO-BYTE ADDITION

A paper-and-pencil addition of two-byte numbers will help us decide how to write a program to perform the operation on the computer. Suppose we want to add these two-byte hex numbers.

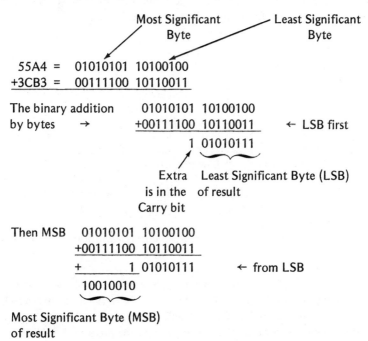

Most Significant
Byte

Least Significant
Byte

55A4 = 01010101 10100100
+3CB3 = 00111100 10110011

The binary addition   01010101 10100100
by bytes   →   +00111100 10110011   ← LSB first
                              1 01010111

Extra   Least Significant Byte (LSB)
is in the   of result
Carry bit

Then MSB   01010101 10100100
           +00111100 10110011
           +   1 01010111   ← from LSB
            10010010

Most Significant Byte (MSB)
of result

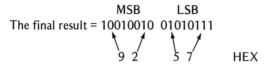

Notice that in this example a carry results from the addition of the Least Significant Bytes. The ADC (ADd with Carry) instruction will automatically add in this carry bit to the sum of the Most Significant Bytes. Therefore, it appears that the two-byte numbers are summed by adding first, the Least Significant Bytes and second, the Most Significant Bytes.

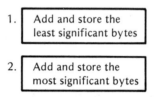

Figure 9-1. Functional Blocks for Addition

It looks like a very straightforward program. Set up a block of memory to store the bytes that are to be added and the bytes of the result of the addition. Since there are two bytes for each number, set aside 6 bytes.

Memory location		Value stored
1100		LSB of 1st number
1101		MSB of 1st number
1102		LSB of 2nd number
1103		MSB of 2nd number
1104		MSB of result ⎫ ← The order of
1105		LSB of result ⎭ the result is reversed for convenience of display

Figure 9-2. Storage for Two-Byte Addition

The first two-byte number to be added is stored in memory location 1100 (Least Significant Byte) and 1101 (Most Significant Byte). The second number is stored in memory location 1102 (Least Significant Byte) and 1103 (Most Significant Byte). These values must all be loaded *before* the program is executed. You know how to do this in the Debugger mode.

Break down the functional blocks into detailed steps and use the mnemonic instructions that you have become familiar with.

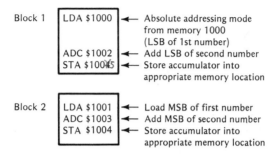

Figure 9-3. Detailed Steps for Functional Blocks

One thing that you must remember about the ADC instruction is that the Carry bit (if set) is added to the sum. When you add the Least Significant Bytes, you must be sure that the carry bit is off (reset to zero). Therefore, a CLC (Clear Carry bit) is needed before the Least Significant Bytes are added.

If you draw a flowchart of the operations that must be performed it will help you write the program step by step.

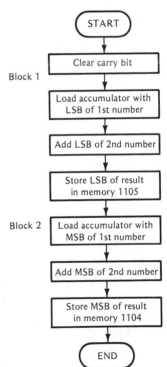

Figure 9-4. Flowchart for Two-Byte Addition

If a program is short, like this one, and you have a detailed flowchart, as in Figure 9-4, you can write the program directly from the flowchart in the Writer/Editor mode.

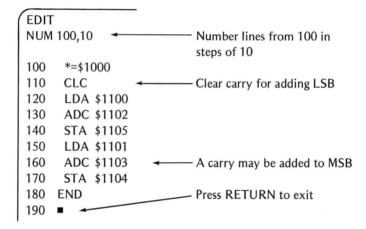

```
EDIT
NUM 100,10          ◄─────────── Number lines from 100 in
                                 steps of 10
100    *=$1000
110    CLC          ◄─────────── Clear carry for adding LSB
120    LDA $1100
130    ADC $1102
140    STA $1105
150    LDA $1101
160    ADC $1103    ◄─────────── A carry may be added to MSB
170    STA $1104
180 END                          Press RETURN to exit
190 ■    ◄─────────────
```

Notice that LDA, ADC, and STA are all used in the Absolute Addressing mode this time. You can use that mode since you know exactly where each piece of data is in memory or where you wish to put it in memory.

Once the program has been entered, assemble it.

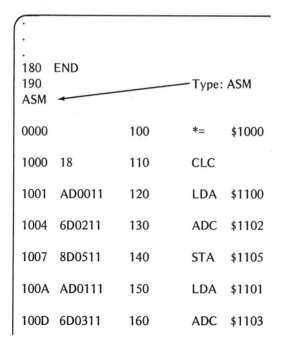

```
        .
        .
        .
180   END
190                     ─── Type: ASM
ASM   ◄───────────

0000              100      *=      $1000

1000   18        110      CLC

1001  AD0011     120      LDA     $1100

1004  6D0211     130      ADC     $1102

1007  8D0511     140      STA     $1105

100A  AD0111     150      LDA     $1101

100D  6D0311     160      ADC     $1103
```

1010   8D0411   170   STA $1104

180 END

EDIT
∎

Now, the program is assembled. It resides in memory locations 1000 through 1012. Don't forget the data. Use the data shown in the paper-and-pencil example so that you can check the results:

$$\begin{array}{r} 55A4 \\ +3CB3 \\ \hline 9257 \end{array}$$

Place the four pieces of data in the four specified memory locations.

MEMORY	Data	
1100	A4	LSB 1st number
1101	55	MSB 1st number
1102	B3	LSB 2nd number
1103	3C	MSB 2nd number

Figure 9-5. Data Used in Example

You are now ready to go to the Debugger mode to enter the data into the memory locations shown in Figure 9-5. Remember how to do it with the Change Memory command?

```
        .
        .
        .
EDIT
BUG

DEBUG                          All four pieces in
C1100<A4,55,B3,3C              consecutive memory
∎                              locations
```

Now execute the program and display memory locations 1104 and 1005 to see the sum.

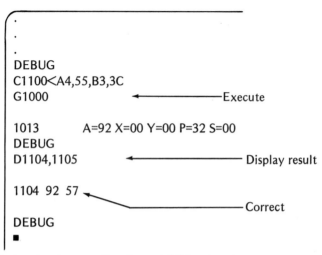

Before leaving the **Two-Byte Addition Program,** try adding the pairs of numbers given in Figure 9-6. Use the Change Memory command to put the numbers in memory. Place your answers in the appropriate boxes in Figure 9-6. Check your results against the answers given in the answers to chapter exercises.

First Number	Second Number	Sum
000A	000B	
13C5	0F24	
6666	333E	
37AB	A09D	
E111	2000	

Figure 9-6. Two-Byte Addition Exercises

Beware of the last exercise in Figure 9-6. Can you tell what result will be displayed after the program has been executed?

TWO PROGRAMS IN MEMORY

Suppose you wish to have an addition program and a subtraction program in the computer at the same time. Only three changes are necessary to convert the addition program now in the computer, to a two-byte subtraction program. It would be time consuming to rewrite the program, but you can quickly copy the addition program to a different block of memory with the DEBUGGER's

Move command. Then you can modify the original addition program to perform subtraction instead.

You have probably noticed that a BRK instruction (Op Code 00) is inserted at the end of each program when it is assembled. The END statement of the **Source Program** creates the BRK statement. The BRK instruction should be included as you move the original program.

.	.
.	.
1000	18
1001	AD
.	.
.	.
.	.
1012	11
1013	00

Original addition program

.	.
.	.
.	.
1020	18
1021	AD
.	.
.	.
.	.
1032	11
1033	00

Move original program to these locations

.	.
.	.

If you don't remember how to use the Move command, see Chapter 6 or follow this procedure:

```
.
.
.
1104  92  57              ← Answer from addition

DEBUG
M1020<1000,1013           ← Move

DEBUG
■
```

Verify that the two programs are the same before going on to be sure that the move was made correctly.

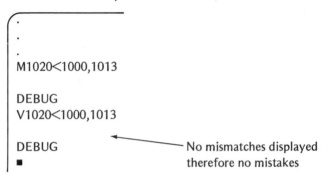

```
.
.
.
M1020<1000,1013

DEBUG
V1020<1000,1013

DEBUG                              ←─────────── No mismatches displayed
■                                               therefore no mistakes
```

Now, you're ready to change the original program so that it will subtract instead of add.

TWO-BYTE SUBTRACTION

Subtraction of two-byte numbers is performed in a similar manner. The **Two-Byte Addition Program** can be modified by three minor changes:

- At memory location 1000:
  change 18 (CLC) to 38 (SEC) ← Set the carry bit instead of clearing it
- At memory locations 1004 *and* 100D:
  change 6D (ADC) to ED (SBC) ← Subtract with borrow instead of add with carry

The change at 1000 sets the carry bit in preparation for the subtraction just as it did the **One-Byte Subtraction Program** of Chapter 4. The add with carry instruction (ADC) is replaced by the subtract with borrow (SBC). The subtract instruction is used in the Absolute Addressing mode. The address which contains the number to be subtracted follows the Op Code, as it followed the ADC instruction in the addition program. Thus, the Least Significant Byte of the value to be subtracted is contained in address 1102. The Most Significant Byte of the value to be subtracted is contained in address 1103.

The changes:

```
.
.
V1020<1000,1013

DEBUG
C1000<38
C1004<ED
C100D<ED
■
```

You now have two machine language programs in the computer. The **Two-Byte Addition Program** was assembled starting at location 1000 but was moved to 1020 through 1032. The **Two-Byte Subtraction Program** is now in locations 1000 through 1013. You can now use either program by choosing the correct memory address for the G command which executes the program starting at the location that you specify.

Before you execute either program, put the original numbers (55A4 and 3CB3) back into memory locations 1100 through 1103.

```
.
.
.
C1100<A4,55,B3,3C          ← Be sure you use the
■                            correct order
```

You can now use either program.

```
.
.
.
G1000                      ← First use subtraction

1013      A=18 X=00 Y=00 P=32 S=00
DEBUG
D1104,1105

1104  18  F1               ← Answer: 18F1 for subtraction

DEBUG
■
```

```
1104  18  F1

DEBUG
G1020                      ← Now addition

1033      A=92 X=00 Y=00 P=32 S=00
DEBUG
D1104,1105                 ← Display result

1104  92  57               ── Answer: 9257 for addition

DEBUG
■
```

Check the subtraction with paper and pencil to make sure that the subtraction result is correct. We hope you like binary subtraction. There are lots of borrows.

```
 55A4 =  0101 0101 1010 0100
-3CB3 =  0011 1100 1011 0011
         0001 1000 1111 0001    binary
      =   1    8    F    1      hex         Yes, it checks
```

Try the subtraction exercises in Figure 9-7. Watch the result of the last two exercises in the table. Can you explain the results?

First Number	Last Number	Difference
FFFF	0112	
76A3	6DCB	
590A	3A1B	
2222	3333	
0000	0004	

Figure 9-7. Two-Byte Subtraction Exercises

The problem involved with the last two exercises in Figure 9-7 is that you are trying to subtract a positive number from a smaller positive number.

```
  2222       and      0000
 -3333               -0004
```

Algebra students know that the result of each of these exercises is a negative number. You actually saw these results displayed on the screen.

```
     EEEF      and      FFFC
```

This means that a method must exist to determine whether a number is positive or negative.

NEGATIVE NUMBERS

It is possible to look at the way data is represented in the computer in a different way. If signed numbers (those that are either positive, negative, or zero) are to be represented, the computer must have some way to tell them apart.

Consider an 8-bit block of data as being composed of one sign bit and seven data bits.

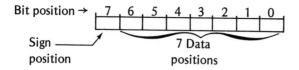

1. If the sign position holds a zero, the data is considered to be a positive number.

Examples:

```
0 1 1 1 1 1 1 1  =  +127 (64+32+16+8+4+2+1)
0 1 1 1 1 1 1 0  =  +126 (64+32+16+8+4+2  )
0 1 1 1 1 1 0 1  =  +125 (64+32+16+8+4   +1)
0 1 1 1 1 1 0 0  =  +124 (64+32+16+8+4      )
              .                .              .
              .                .              .
              .                .              .
              .                .              .
              .                .              .
0 0 0 0 0 0 1 1  =  +3  (                +2+1)
0 0 0 0 0 0 1 0  =  +2  (                +2  )
0 0 0 0 0 0 0 1  =  +1  (                  +1)
0 0 0 0 0 0 0 0  =  +0  (                    )
```

Zero is considered a positive
number by Branch Instructions

2. If the sign position holds a one (1), the data is considered to be a negative number.

Examples:

```
1 0 0 0 0 0 0 0  =  -128
1 0 0 0 0 0 0 1  =  -127
1 0 0 0 0 0 1 0  =  -126
1 0 0 0 0 0 1 1  =  -125
1 0 0 0 0 1 0 0  =  -124
              .
              .
              .
1 1 1 1 1 0 1 1  =  -5
1 1 1 1 1 1 0 0  =  -4
1 1 1 1 1 1 0 1  =  -3
1 1 1 1 1 1 1 0  =  -2
1 1 1 1 1 1 1 1  =  -1
```

We have learned to interpret positive binary numbers as positive decimal numbers, but what about these negative critters? They don't look familiar at all. However, it is plain to see that each 8-bit code could represent all the integers from –128 through +127.

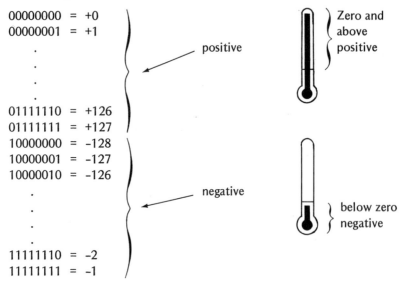

```
00000000 = +0
00000001 = +1
     .
     .
     .
     .
01111110 = +126
01111111 = +127
10000000 = -128
10000001 = -127
10000010 = -126
     .
     .
     .
     .
11111110 = -2
11111111 = -1
```

positive   Zero and
                                   above
                                   positive

negative   below zero
                                   negative

Let's take a look at the negatives and see if there is any meaningful relationship to their positive counterparts.

Consider the positive number 126	=	01111110.
Its one's complement	=	10000001
Its two's complement	=	10000010
Compare the latter with –126	=	10000010

The binary representation of a negative number (–1 through –127) is equal to the two's complement of its positive counterpart.

–127 = the two's complement of +127
–126 = the two's complement of +126
–125 = the two's complement of +125

–2 = the two's complement of +2
–1 = the two's complement of +1

Therefore, you can interpret the form of the results of the last two examples in Figure 9-7 by converting the displayed results as follows:

1. 2222
   -3333

   EEEF hex =   1110 1110 1110 1111   binary
   take the one's
   complement   0001 0001 0001 0000
   add one for the
   two's complement 0001 0001 0001 0001
   Therefore, EEEF hex = negative 1111 hex

2. 0000
   -0004

   FFFC hex =   1111 1111 1111 1100   binary
   one's
   complement   0000 0000 0000 0011
   two's
   complement   0000 0000 0000 0100
   Therefore, FFFC hex = negative 0004 hex

When thinking in terms of signed two-byte hex numbers, all numbers from 8000 through FFFF are considered negative. All two-bytes hex numbers from 0000 through 7FFF, are considered positive.

Unsigned Value	Signed Value	
0001	+0001	
0002	+0002	
0003	+0003	
.	.	
.	.	
.	.	Positive
.	.	
.	.	
7FFD	+7FFD	
7FFE	+7FFE	
7FFF	+7FFF	
8000	-8000	
8001	-7FFF	
8002	-7FFE	
8003	-7FFD	
.	.	
.	.	
.	.	Negative
.	.	
.	.	
FFFD	-0003	
FFFE	-0002	
FFFF	-0001	

Figure 9-8. Two-Byte Hex Signed Numbers

For two-byte numbers, the sign position is considered to be in the *Most Significant Bit* of the *Most Significant Byte*.

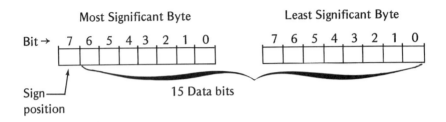

Most Significant Byte   Least Significant Byte

Bit →

Sign position

15 Data bits

Thus numbers such as:

0000000000010000 = 0010 hex
0010011111100110 = 27E6 hex
0110111110101001 = 6FA9 hex

would be interpreted as positive numbers, but numbers such as:

1000000000000000 = 8000 hex
1010011111100101 = A7E5 hex
1111011010111100 = F6BC hex

would be interpreted as negative numbers.

A complete discussion of the arithmetic of signed numbers is beyond the scope of this book. A more thorough discussion of signed numbers and signed number arithmetic can be found in the MOS Technology Programming Manual available in some computer stores or from MOS Technology, Inc., 950 Rittenhouse Road, Norristown, PA 19401.

For our purposes, we must realize that certain branch instructions test the result of numbers to see whether they are negative or positive. This determination depends on whether or not the Negative flag of the Processor Status Register has been set to 1 or not. The Negative flag is set to 1 when the computer interprets the results of certain instructions as negative numbers (a 1 in bit 7 resulting from the operation performed by the instruction). In Chapter 5, a table shows the effect that each instruction has on the various flags in the Processor Status Register.

MULTIPLE-BYTE ADDITION AND SUBTRACTION

To add or subtract numbers that require more than two bytes, an extension of this two-byte procedure can be made. The operation is always performed from the Least Significant Byte forward (or from right to left).

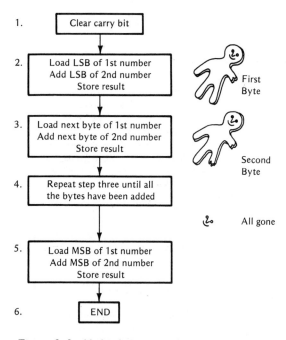

Figure 9-9. Multiple-Byte Addition Flowchart

DECIMAL ARITHMETIC

Are you tired of converting binary to hex to decimal? If so, the 6502 instruction set includes an instruction to help you out. If you are careful to express the values that you wish to add or subtract as *binary-coded-decimal* (BCD) numbers, the Atari can add or subtract those numbers and express the result as a decimal value. What are binary-coded decimal numbers? That's just a fancy name for a binary number that has been separated into two 4-bit parts. These parts are then interpreted as decimal digits.

Examples:

Binary	Binary-coded-decimal	Decimal
01011000	0101 1000	58
10010011	1001 0011	93
00010110	0001 0110	16

Since each four bits is interpreted as a decimal digit, the binary inputs must be chosen with care.

11001001 = 1100 1001
——————————— NOT a BCD value

10101011 = 1010 1011
——————————— NOT BCD values

Each 4-bit part must be one of these:

BCD	DECIMAL
0000	0
0001	1
0010	2
0011	3
0100	4
0101	5
0110	6
0111	7
1000	8
1001	9

The instruction needed to request the computer to perform decimal addition or subtraction is:

SED   (SEt Decimal mode)
   Op Code = F8
      Implied Addressing mode
      One byte long.
      Status flags affected: D

This instruction sets the Decimal flag in the Processor Status Register to 1.

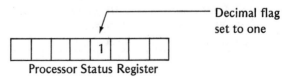

Decimal flag set to one

Processor Status Register

Once this instruction has been used, all of the Add and Subtract instructions will be carried out as decimal operations because of the status of the Decimal flag. The operation of any of the other instructions are *not* affected. If the SED instruction has been executed in a program, and a binary addition or subtraction is desired, the computer must execute the Clear Decimal mode instruction.

CLD   (CLear Decimal mode)
   Op Code = D8
        Implied Addressing mode
        One byte long
        Status flags affected: D

This instruction resets the decimal flag in the Processor Status Register to zero.

Suppose that you want to add the decimal numbers 18 and 23. You might use this program.

ADD TWO DECIMAL NUMBERS

SED   Set decimal mode
CLC   Clear the carry bit
LDA$1000   Load accumulator from memory location $1000
ADC$1001   Add value from memory location $1001
STA $1100   Store the sum

Enter and assemble:

```
.
.
EDIT
NUM 100,10

100     *=$1000                  ← Enter it
110     SED
120     CLC
130     LDA   $1100
140     ADC   $1101
150     STA   $1002
160  END
170
ASM                        ← Assemble it

0000                100     *=$1000
```

```
1000   F8           110    SED

1001   18           120    CLC

1002   AD0011       130    LDA   $1000

1005   6D0111       140    ADC   $1001

1008   8D0211       150    STA   $1002

                    160 END

EDIT
■
```

Go to the DEBUGGER, execute the program, and display the result. Be sure to load the data in 1100 and 1101 first.

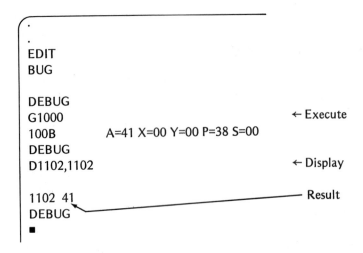

```
.
.
.
EDIT
BUG

DEBUG
G1000                                          ← Execute
100B        A=41 X=00 Y=00 P=38 S=00
DEBUG
D1102,1102                                      ← Display

1102  41 ─────────────────────────── Result
DEBUG
■
```

The decimal result of 18+23 is 41. If we had been adding the hexadecimal values of 18 and 23, the result would have been 3B. Remember, 18 and 23 in hexadecimal notation are different values than 18 and 23 in decimal notation.

3B hex and 41 decimal are *not* equivalent values

Now let's execute the program starting from location 1001 (omitting the Set Decimal instruction) and observe the result.

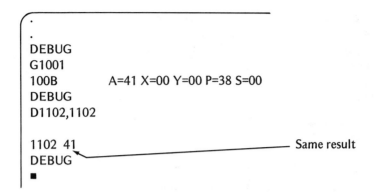

```
.
.
DEBUG
G1001
100B          A=41 X=00 Y=00 P=38 S=00
DEBUG
D1102,1102

1102 41                                        ———— Same result
DEBUG
■
```

> Once the SED instruction has been executed, all additions in the program are performed in the decimal mode. The CLD (Clear Decimal mode) instruction must be executed to get back to binary addition.

The advantage of decimal addition is that it relieves you of converting numbers from one base to another for interpretation. You can enter decimal values (such as 23 and 18) and obtain decimal results (41).

Try the **Add Two Decimal Numbers Program** with other pairs of decimal values. Substitute them for the values that you originally put in memory locations 1100 and 1102. Use the Change Memory command to input the values in Figure 9-10.

The first change would be:

```
.
.
C1100<51,23
■
```

First Number	Second Number	Sum Displayed
51	23	
68	14	
29	17	
33	99	
72	45	

Figure 9-10. Decimal Addition Exercises

What is wrong with the last two exercises in Figure 9-10? Make sure that the sum of the two numbers is less than 100 in this program. Any sum whose value is greater than 99 will not fit in the accumulator or any memory location. Remember, this is an 8-bit computer. Here is what will happen to you if you insist on experimenting (we secretly encourage you).

Last exercise example:

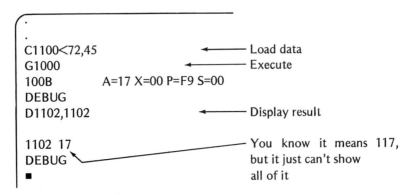

Since the 6502 microprocessor handles blocks of data in 8-bit sizes, some provision must be made for the situation which results when a sum is larger than can be held in 8 bits. This technique was shown in earlier chapters with hexadecimal arithmetic. The same method will work with decimal addition and subtraction.

SUMMARY

In this chapter you have learned:

- To break large numbers into more than one byte in order to perform two-byte arithmetic,
- To retrieve, add (or subtract), and store separate bytes of two-byte numbers using the Absolute Addressing mode,
- How the carry flag is used for two-byte addition and subtraction,
- How to move blocks of data from one area of memory to another,
- How signed numbers may be interpreted:
  negative if Most Significant Bit is set to 1
  positive if Most Significant Bit is reset to 0,
- The significance of the status flags on the Processor Status Register for branch instructions,
- That addition and subtraction can be performed on numbers larger than two bytes,

- To write numbers in binary-coded-decimal (BCD) form so that the computer can perform decimal addition and subtraction,
- How to use the Set Decimal mode and Clear Decimal mode to perform either decimal or binary arithmetic.

EXERCISES

1. If the two-byte hex numbers 9B and 66 are added, will the sum be too large to be held in the accumulator? _____

2. Tell how the computer will handle the sum in Exercise 1.
   (a) Number in accumulator _____
   (b) The Carry flag will be_____
                         (zero, one)

3. The following data is stored (or to be stored) in the specified memory locations.

Address	Data
1100	3F
1111	A3
1112		← Put sum here

   Give the assembly language instructions to load the number from address 1110, add the number from address 1111 and store the result using the Absolute Addressing mode.
   (a) _____
   (b) _____
   (c) _____

4. In performing an addition or subtraction operation on the Least Significant Bytes, the Carry flag must be appropriately set *or* reset. The assembly instruction:
   (a) for addition is _____
   (b) for subtraction is _____

5. Show where the data would be placed by the following instruction.
   C1120<15,A4,32,CC

Address	Data
1120	
1121	
1122	
1123	

6. Write the DEBUGGER command that would move the data from where it is in memory in Exercise 5 to memory block 1105 through 1108.

_____

7. Tell whether the following *signed* numbers would be interpreted as negative *or* positive.
   (a) 10100111 binary _____
   (b) 7F hex _____
   (c) 01011111 binary_____
   (d) A3 hex _____

8. Two-byte signed numbers are considered:
   (a) positive if in the range of _____ through _____
   (b) negative if in the range of_____ through_____

ANSWERS

Figure 9-6

First Number	Second Number	Sum
000A	000B	0015
13C5	0F24	22E9
6666	333E	99A4
37AB	A09D	D848
E111	2000	0111

Most Significant Bit is lost

Figure 9-7

First Number	Last Number	Difference
FFFF	0112	FEED
76A3	6DCB	08D8
590A	3A1B	1EEF
2222	3333	EEEF
0000	0004	FFFC

Last two are negative results

Figure 9-10

First Number	Second Number	Sum Displayed
51	23	74
68	14	82
29	17	46
33	99	32
72	45	17

Most Significant Bit is
lost in last two answers

1. yes

2. (a) 01
   (b) one   (true answer is 101)

3. (a) LDA $1110
   (b) ADC $1111
   (c) STA $1112

4. (a) CLC
   (b) SEC

5.

Address	Data
1120	15
1121	A4
1122	32
1123	CC

6. M1105<1120,1123

7. (a) negative
   (b) positive
   (c) positive
   (d) negative

8. (a) 0000 through 7FFF
   (b) 8000 through FFFF

Chapter 10

Shift and Rotate

You learned to add and subtract in Chapter 9, but these two operations are only half of the four basic arithmetic operations. What about multiplication and division? The 6502 microprocessor has no instructions that will directly perform multiplication and division. However, think of the way that you perform these operations with pencil and paper.

You perform a series of additions, subtractions, and shifts to get the partial answers into the correct place value.

Examples:

(a) Multiplication

```
    23
  x 32
    46 ◄─────── 1)  Two 23's = 23+23 = 46
    69 ◄─────── 2)  Shift one place left
  ───────────── 3)  Three 23's = 23+23+23 = 69
   736          4)  Add 46+69 = 736
```

(b) Division

```
        32
    23) 736
        69 ◄─── 1)  Three 23's = 23+23+23 = 69
           ──── 2)  Subtract
        46 ◄─── 3)  Shift right and bring down
        46 ◄─── 4)  Two 23's = 23+23 = 46
         0 ◄─── 5)  Subtract
```

You know that the computer can add and subtract, but you must learn how to manipulate numbers with instructions that will shift the numbers left or right before you tackle the multiplication and division operations.

Let's take another look at the structure of 8-bit binary numbers so that you can better understand the consequences of changing place values.

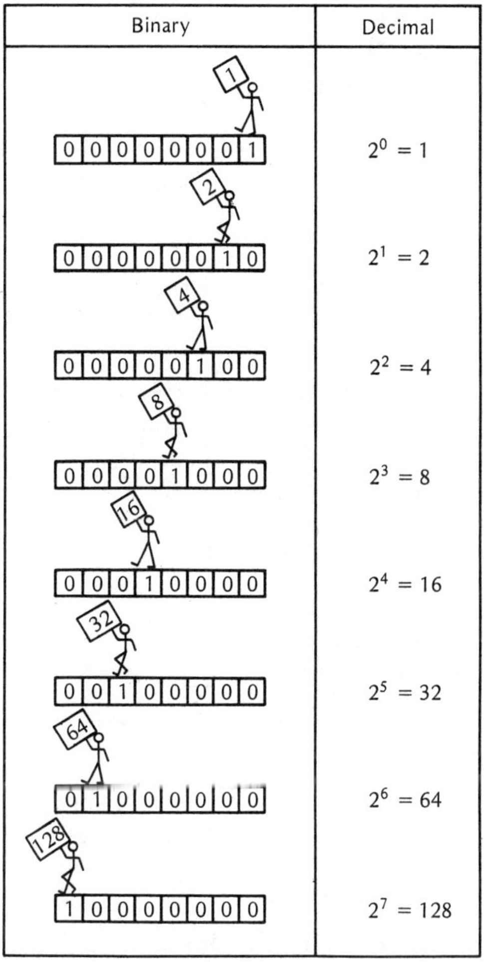

Binary	Decimal
0 0 0 0 0 0 0 1	$2^0 = 1$
0 0 0 0 0 0 1 0	$2^1 = 2$
0 0 0 0 0 1 0 0	$2^2 = 4$
0 0 0 0 1 0 0 0	$2^3 = 8$
0 0 0 1 0 0 0 0	$2^4 = 16$
0 0 1 0 0 0 0 0	$2^5 = 32$
0 1 0 0 0 0 0 0	$2^6 = 64$
1 0 0 0 0 0 0 0	$2^7 = 128$

Figure 10-1. 8-bit Binary Place Values

You can see from Figure 10-1 that each place value is double that of the place value immediately to its right. In other words, shifting a binary digit one place to the left doubles its value.

Study the following examples which demonstrate the results of a single shift left for each digit.

	Binary	Hex	Decimal
1.	00000101	5	5
Shifted	00001010	A	10

2.	Binary	Hex	Decimal
	00000111	7	7
Shifted	00001110	E	14
3.	Binary	Hex	Decimal
	00010010	12	18
Shifted	00100100	24	36
4.	Binary	Hex	Decimal
	01101001	69	105
Shifted	11010010	D2	210

From the previous examples, you can see that a shift of one place to the left doubles the value of an 8-bit number. In the decimal paper-and-pencil multiplication and division examples, you made shifts which changed the place values by powers of ten.

```
    23
  x 32
    46 ◄——————— 2 x 23
    69 ◄————————— shift left a power of ten because 3x 23 is really 30x 23
   736
```

In binary multiplication:

```
   101
  x 11
   101◄——————— 1 x 101
   101          Shift left a power of two because
  1111          1 x 101 is really 10 x 101
```

You really do it in two parts

```
   101          101
  x  1         x 10
   101    +    1010    =    1111
```

The shifting is just a short cut to perform separate operations as one unit.

In this chapter, we will describe the four shift and rotate instructions in the 6502 instruction set. We will also use subroutines, short mini-programs that can be branched to from several different locations.

First, we will demonstrate how the shift and rotate instructions work and then show some applications.

The four instructions are:

1. ASL (Arithmetic Shift Left),
2. LSR (Logical Shift Right),
3. ROL (ROtate Left), and
4. ROR (ROtate Right).

ARITHMETIC SHIFT LEFT

The first instruction that we will look at is ASL. This instruction shifts every bit in a particular byte of data one position to the left, as we have been discussing in previous examples.

One thing we didn't discuss earlier. If the 8 bits are shifted left, what happens at each end?

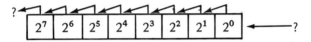

The 2^0 bit goes to 2^1
   2^1 bit goes to 2^2
   2^2 bit goes to 2^3
   2^3 bit goes to 2^4
   2^4 bit goes to 2^5
   2^5 bit goes to 2^6
   2^6 bit goes to 2^7
But where does the 2^7 bit go, and where does the 2^0 bit come from?

Each time that the ASL instruction is executed, the Carry flag assumes the value that was in the leftmost bit (2^7) before the shift occurred. All the rest of the bits are moved left one position, and a zero is moved into the rightmost position (2^0).

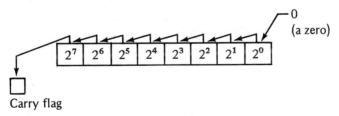

Carry flag

Here is an example that shows the contents of the accumulator before, during, and after the instruction is executed. The value, B1, is in the accumulator before execution.

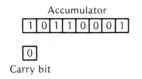

Figure 10-2(a). Before ASL

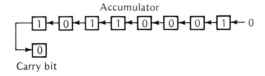

Figure 10-2(b). This Is What Happens

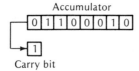

Figure 10-2(c). After ASL

Enter the following short little program, and you can see the computer shift the value in the accumulator when the ASL instruction is executed. The program places a one in the accumulator and shifts it left one place.

```
.
.
EDIT
NUM 100,10

100    *=$1000
110    CLC
120    LDA #1      ◄──── Load a 1 (00000001 binary)
130    ASL  A      ◄──── Shift left once
140    END
150    ■
```

Assemble the program.

```
.
.
150
ASM

0000          100      *=    $1000
1000  18      110      CLC
1001  A901    120      LDA   #$01
1003  0A      130      ASL   A
              140 END

EDIT
■
```

Now, enter the DEBUGGER and set the accumulator to zero by using the Charge Register command.

```
.
.
EDIT
BUG

DEBUG
CR<0
■
```

Trace the program by typing: T1000 and pressing the RETURN key.

```
                .
                .
                T1000
                1000  18          CLC            Accumulator
                    A=00 X=00 Y=00 P=32 S=00     00000000
                1001  A9 01       LDA   #$01
See the             A=01 X=00 Y=00 P=30 S=00     00000001
Accum.          1003  0A          ASL   A
                    A=02 X=00 Y=00 P=30 S=00     00000010
Now             1004  00          BRK
shifted             A=02 X=00 Y=00 P=30 S=00

                DEBUG
                ■
```

Now, reset the accumulator to zero before going on to the next program.

```
DEBUG
CR<0
```

You only shifted left one time in the previous program. What happens if you shift left 8 times in succession? Would there be anything left in the accumulator? What would be the condition of the Carry flag? Try it.

Enter the program shown below and assemble it.

```
010    *=$1000
020    CLC
030    LDA #1
040    ASL A
050    ASL A
060    ASL A
070    ASL A          8 Left shifts
080    ASL A
090    ASL A
100    ASL A
110    ASL A
120    END
```

This program sets the carry bit to zero, puts a 1 in the accumulator, and shifts the accumulator left 8 times. When the program is done, the accumulator should be zero and the Carry flag should be set, because the bit which forms the 1 in the accumulator was shifted left through every bit and then out of the accumulator and into the Carry bit. To see this for yourself, type "BUG" and press RETURN. Then type "DR" and press RETURN again. You should see the registers as they are below.

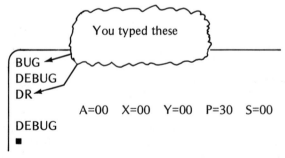

```
You typed these

BUG
DEBUG
DR
          A=00   X=00   Y=00   P=30   S=00
DEBUG
■
```

The accumulator is zero, and as you can see, the Carry bit is not set in the Processor Status Register (P).

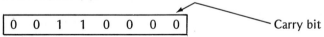

| 0 | 0 | 1 | 1 | 0 | 0 | 0 | 0 | Carry bit

Processor Status Register = 30 hex

Now, execute the program by typing: G1000, and press the RETURN key. You should see the following:

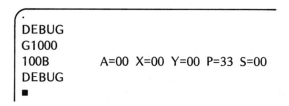

```
DEBUG
G1000
100B          A=00 X=00 Y=00 P=33 S=00
DEBUG
■
```

The Processor Status Register has changed, and the Carry flag (bit 0) is set.

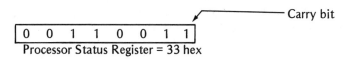

```
                                        ─── Carry bit
| 0   0   1   1   0   0   1   1 |
Processor Status Register = 33 hex
```

Now try typing "T1000" to Trace the program. You will be able to see the registers as they are changing after each step in the program. Be sure to press RETURN after typing "T1000".

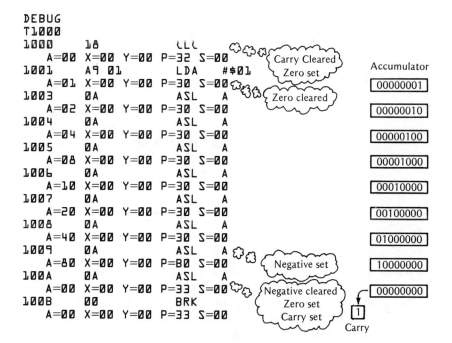

Figure 10-3. Trace of the Shift Program

After the first instruction of the program (CLC) is executed, the Processor Status Register (P register) shows a value of 32. This means the Carry flag is zero. If a carry had occurred, the P register would read 33. Note that the Zero flag (bit 1 of the P register) is set.

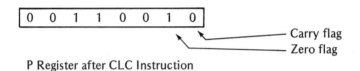

Carry flag
Zero flag

P Register after CLC Instruction

After the next step (LDA #$01), which loads the 1 into the accumulator, the A register = 01 and P=30, indicating that when the 1 (a non-zero value) was loaded, the Zero bit was turned off.

A Register   P Register

- Note the pattern in the accumulator after each left shift. As the original 1 is shifted, the value in the accumulator is effectively doubled.

- Notice that when the value of 80 was in the accumulator, the P register changed to B0. When a value greater than 7F results from a shift, the Negative flag (bit 7 of the P register) is turned on. As you found out earlier in the book, the computer considers any number with its 7th bit on (all hex numbers between 80 and FF) as negative for comparing purposes (such as those used by branches).

After the last shift instruction is performed, the A register becomes zero and the bit that formed the value of 80 has been moved over to the Carry bit of the P register. The Negative flag is off (since the A register is zero). This leaves the P register with its Carry and Zero bits set to 1.

A Register   P Register

As we mentioned earlier, shifting a number left has the effect of doubling that number. This can be used to make a simple multiplication program. This program can only multiply a number by a multiple of two, though. If you want to multiply a number by 2, shift it once. You shift it twice to multiply by 4, three times for 8, etc. The program shown below is an example of multiplying 8 by 4. Enter the program and assemble.

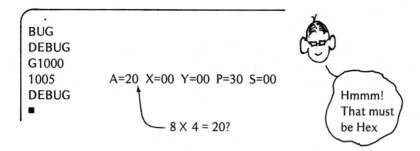

```
010    *=$1000
020    CLC
030    LDA    #8
040    ASL    A    ←—— Doubled
050    ASL    A    ←—— and redoubled
060    END
```

Now enter DEBUG and run it.

```
BUG
DEBUG
G1000
1005      A=20  X=00  Y=00  P=30  S=00
DEBUG
■
                8 X 4 = 20?
```

Hmmm! That must be Hex

The accumulator now holds the number 20 (hex), which is the same as 32 in decimal, 8x 4=32, right?

You have to be careful when you multiply numbers this way, though, because if you have a number like 80 (hex), and you try to multiply it by 4 by shifting it left twice, you are going to get an answer of zero in the accumulator and the Carry bit.

Accumulator

1	0	0	0	0	0	0	0

| 0 |
Carry bit

Figure 10-4(a). Original Value

Accumulator

0	0	0	0	0	0	0	0

| 1 |
Carry bit

Figure 10-4(b). After One Shift

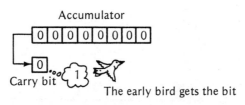

Accumulator

0	0	0	0	0	0	0	0

| 0 |
Carry bit

The early bird gets the bit

Figure 10-4(c). After Two Shifts

We have used the ASL instruction in the Accumulator Addressing mode. This instruction as well as the other shift and rotate instructions may be used in that mode or the Zero Page, Zero Page Indexed, the Absolute, or the Absolute indexed mode as indicated in the tables in Chapter 5.

The ASL instruction, as well as other shift and rotate instructions affect the Negative, Zero, and Carry flags in the Processor Status Register when they are executed.

LOGICAL SHIFT RIGHT

The LSR (Logical Shift Right) instruction, despite the word "Logical" rather than "Arithmetic," does the same thing as the ASL, except in the opposite direction. Each time it is executed, a zero is moved into the leftmost bit, the rest of the bits are shifted to the right, and the rightmost bit goes over into the Carry flag.

Accumulator

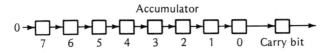

7   6   5   4   3   2   1   0   Carry bit

Figure 10-5. Operation of LSR

We will demonstrate this instruction by loading a value to be shifted into the accumulator from a memory location, and shift it right a given number of times. After each shift, the value of the accumulator is stored in another memory location. Every shift after the first stores the value in the next highest memory location.

Address	Data
1100	Original value
1101	Number of shifts
1102	Result of 1 shift
1103	Result of 2 shifts
1104	Result of 3 shifts
1105	etc.

Figure 10-6. Memory Use for Shift Right

The program is detailed below.

Instruction	Remarks
*=$1000	Start the program at location 1000
CLC	Clear the Carry bit
LDX #0	Set the memory pointer to zero
LDA $1100	Get the value to be shifted
LDY $1101	Load the number of times that the number is to be shifted into Y
LOOP LSR A	Shift it once
STA $1102,X	Put it in the next memory location
INX	Point to the next location
DEY	Find out if we have shifted enough
BNE LOOP	If not, go back and shift

This program will take the number that you put in location 1100 (hex) and shift it right just as many times as you have told it to in location 1101. The results of each shift will be stored starting in location 1102 and continuing for as many locations as there are shifts. Enter the program below and assemble it.

RIGHT SHIFTER PROGRAM

```
010    *=$1000
020    CLC
030    LDX   #0
040    LDA   $1100
050    LDY   $1101
060    LOOP LSR A
070    STA   $1102,X
080    INX
090    DEY
100    BNE   LOOP
110    END
```

Now enter DEBUG and put any value you want to see shifted into location1100. Suppose the value is 80 (hex). You would enter:

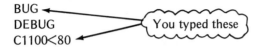

```
BUG
DEBUG
C1100<80
```
You typed these

Now enter the number of times that you want the number to be shifted into location 1101. Suppose it is 7. You type:

C1101<07

You now have:

Address	Data
1100	80
1101	07

Now you are ready to run the program. Type: G1000, and press the RETURN key. To see the results, type D1102,1108. This will let you look at the seven locations used to store the shifted values.

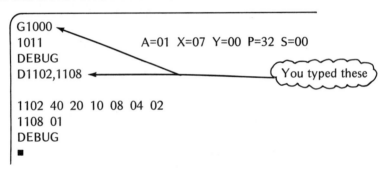

```
G1000
1011                  A=01  X=07  Y=00  P=32  S=00
DEBUG
D1102,1108                                            You typed these

1102 40 20 10 08 04 02
1108 01
DEBUG
■
```

And there they are! Note the values in the registers when the program was finished:

- The accumulator contains the last shifted result.
- The X register contains the number of times that the accumulator was shifted.
- The Y register is zero, indicating that all 7 shifts have been performed.
- The P register shows that the Carry flag is not set. That is because there were not enough shifts made for the one to be bumped over into the Carry bit.

If you could see the data in memory locations 1102 through 1108 in binary form, the shifts would be more apparent.

Address	Binary Data
1102	01000000
1103	00100000
1104	00010000
1105	00001000
1106	00000100
1107	00000010
1108	00000001

Now try shifting 8 times and see what happens. Change memory location 1101 and execute the program again. Display memory locations 1102 through 1109 this time.

```
C1101<8
G1000
1011        A=00 X=08 Y=00 P=33 S=00
D1102,1109

1102 40 20 10 08 04 02
1108 01 00
DEBUG
■
```

Notice the P register contains 33 at the end of the run. The Carry bit was turned on by the last shift right.

Show what values would be in the four registers if you executed the program with the following values in memory.

Address	Data
1100	80
1101	0A

A= _____   X= _____   Y= _____   P= _____

Try entering the values in Figure 10-7 at locations 1100 and 1101. Fill in the values in memory at the end of the program's execution.
the values in memory at the end of the program's execution.

(a)

Address	Data
1100	91
1101	03
1102	
1103	
1104	

(b)

Address	Data
1100	33
1101	04
1102	
1103	
1104	
1105	

(c)

Address	Data
1100	E7
1101	06
1102	
1103	
1104	
1105	
1106	
1107	

Figure 10-7. LSR Exercises

The two rotate instructions basically do the same thing as the shift instructions, with one important difference. Instead of throwing out the Carry bit and filling in a zero at one end of the byte, the Carry bit is rotated back into the original byte again.

ROTATE LEFT

The rotate left instruction (ROL) tells the computer to think of data in terms of blocks in a wheel instead of blocks in a straight line.

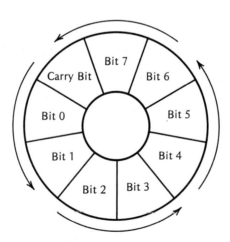

Figure 10-8. Rotate Left Wheel

Or as is more conventional:

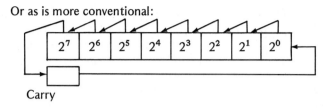

Carry

When a large number of rotations are made in succession, no bits are lost. They merely go round and round to different positions. It's something like the game of musical chairs except that no one takes any of the chairs away. There's always a place for each bit of data to go.

The next program sets the Carry bit and loads the accumulator with 1. Then the accumulator is rotated left eight times. On the last rotate, the Carry bit is set by the 1 that has been rotated through the accumulator. The accumulator ends up with a value of 80 due to the original carry that has rotated through the accumulator.

Enter the program and assemble it.

```
010     *=$1000
020     SEC
030     LDA    #1
040     ROL    A
050     ROL    A
060     ROL    A
070     ROL    A
080     ROL    A
090     ROL    A
100     ROL    A
110     ROL    A
```

Now run the program by entering the Debugger mode and typing: G1000. (Don't forget the RETURN key.) You should see:

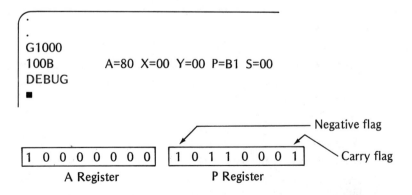

You can see from the P register that the Carry and Negative flags are set. The carry was set when the 1 that we had in the accumulator was shifted all the way over and out of the accumulator and into the Carry bit. The Negative flag was set when the value of the accumulator became C0 (and stayed set for 80) due to the shifting.

Examine the trace of the program that follows.

```
DEBUG
T1000
1000      38              SEC
          A=00 X=00 Y=00 P=31 S=00
1001      A9 01           LDA   #$01
          A=01 X=00 Y=00 P=31 S=00
1003      2A              ROL   A
          A=03 X=00 Y=00 P=30 S=00
1004      2A              ROL   A
          A=06 X=00 Y=00 P=30 S=00
1005      2A              ROL   A
          A=0C X=00 Y=00 P=30 S=00
1006      2A              ROL   A
          A=18 X=00 Y=00 P=30 S=00
1007      2A              ROL   A
          A=30 X=00 Y=00 P=30 S=00
1008      2A              ROL   A
          A=60 X=00 Y=00 P=30 S=00
1009      2A              ROL   A
          A=C0 X=00 Y=00 P=B0 S=00
100A      2A              ROL   A
          A=80 X=00 Y=00 P=B1 S=00
100B      00              BRK
          A=80 X=00 Y=00 P=B1 S=00
DEBUG
■
```

In the first step, the Carry flag is set by the SEC instruction. Then a 1 is loaded into the accumulator. After the first ROL instruction, bit 7 of the accumulator (a zero) has been moved into the Carry bit, resetting it (as shown by P=30). The old value of the Carry bit (a one) is moved into bit 0 of the accumulator. All the rest of the bits in the accumulator have been shifted one position to the left, giving a value of 03 in the accumulator.

Figure 10-9 shows the binary results of each step in the program.

After the seventh rotate instruction has been executed, the accumulator has a value of C0. This sets the Negative flag, making P=B0. After the next ro-

Step	Instruction	Carry	Accumulator
1000	SEC	1	00000000
1001	LDA #01	1	00000001
1003	ROL A	0	00000011
1004	ROL A	0	00000110
1005	ROL A	0	00001100
1006	ROL A	0	00011000
1007	ROL A	0	00110000
1008	ROL A	0	01100000
1009	ROL A	0	11000000
100A	ROL A	1	10000000

This is the way it rotates

the last time around

Figure 10-9. Accumulator and Carry Rotates

tate, bit 7 of the accumulator (a one) gets moved into the Carry bit, setting it and making P=B1. The value, 80, is left in the accumulator.

ROTATE RIGHT

The rotate-right instruction (ROL) works in the opposite direction as rotate left. As successive rotate-right instructions are executed, the bits in the accumulator and carry go around and around clockwise.

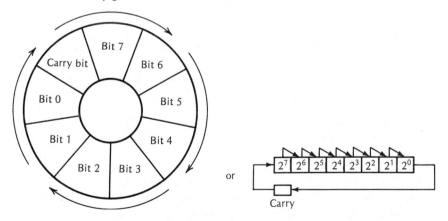

or

Figure 10-10. Rotate–Right Wheel

A rotate-right instruction executed following a rotate-left instruction would put all bits back in their original place.

Example:

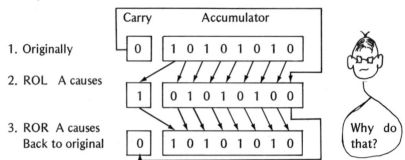

	Carry	Accumulator
1. Originally	0	1 0 1 0 1 0 1 0
2. ROL A causes	1	0 1 0 1 0 1 0 0
3. ROR A causes Back to original	0	1 0 1 0 1 0 1 0

Why do that?

I don't know why anyone would want to do that, but you might think up a reason.

To demonstrate the ROR instruction, look back to the **Right Shifter Program** and see how it might be changed to make it a **Right Rotater Program**. Only this time provide the following initial values:

- Carry bit = 1
- Memory location 1100 = 0
- Memory location 1101 = 0
- Rotate right memory location 1100 8 times
- Store the result of each rotation in successive memory locations from 1111 through 1118

You might do it like this:

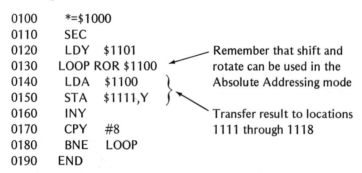

```
0100        *=$1000
0110        SEC
0120        LDY   $1101              Remember that shift and
0130   LOOP ROR $1100                rotate can be used in the
0140        LDA   $1100              Absolute Addressing mode
0150        STA   $1111,Y
0160        INY                      Transfer result to locations
0170        CPY   #8                 1111 through 1118
0180        BNE   LOOP
0190        END
```

We changed the program quite a bit to show you that there's more than one way to achieve the same result. The Y register now serves as a loop counter *and* as an index to store the result of each rotate.

Enter the program and assemble it. Then go to the DEBUGGER to store the initial values in memory.

```
  .
  .
BUG

DEBUG
C1100<0,0  ◄──────── This will set both 1100 and
■                      1101 to zero
```

Single step the program and watch the accumulator change as it is loaded from 1100 each time the instruction at 1007 is executed. Also watch the Y register change at 100D.

```
  .
  .
C1100<0,0
S1000
1000     38              SEC
    A=00 X=00 Y=00 P=33 S=00
DEBUG
S
1001     AC 01 11    LDY      $1101
    A=00 X=00 Y=00 P=33 S=00
DEBUG
S
1004     6E 00 11    ROR      $1100 ◄────── You can't see it
    A=00 X=00 Y=000 P=B0 S=00               do it but . . . . .
DEBUG
S
1007     AD 00 11    LDA      $1100 ┌── there it is
    A=80 X=00 Y=00 P=B0 S=00 ◄──
DEBUG                                  ┌─────────┐
S                                      │10000000 │ Accumulator
100A     99 11 11    STA      $1111,Y  └─────────┘
    A=80 X=00 Y=00 P=B0 S=00
DEBUG
S
100D     4C              INY
    A=80 X=00 Y=01 P=30 S=00 ◄────────── Y changed
```

```
        .
        .
        .
DEBUG
S
100E     CO  08        CPY      #$08
     A=80 X=00 Y=01 P=30 S=00
DEBUG
S
1010     D0  F2        BNE      $1004
     A=80 X=00 Y=01 P=30 S=00
DEBUG
S
1004     6E  00  11    ROR      $1100          Rotate again
     A=80 X=00 Y=01 P=30 S=00
DEBUG
S
1007     AD  00  11    LDA      $1100
     A=40 X=00 Y=01 P=30 S=00              There it is
DEBUG                                      01000000 Accumulator
        .
        .
        .
```

Continue single stepping until the program ends. When finished, display memory locations 1111 through 1118.

```
        .
        .
        .
DEBUG
D1111,1118

1111 80 40 20 10 08 04 02
1118 01

DEBUG
■
```

You are now able to manipulate data in four ways. Proceed to the summary and then the exercises.

SUMMARY

This chapter contains discussions of shift and rotate instructions to prepare you for multiplication and division operations which follow in the next chapter. You learned that:

- Multiplication and division operations are performed by a series of additions, subtractions, and place location shifts;
- Shifting a binary digit left one place doubles the place value of the digit;
- Shifting all bits of a binary number left one place doubles the value of the binary number;
- Shift and rotate instructions may be used in the following address modes;
  Accumulator, Zero Page, Zero Page Indexed, Absolute, and Absolute Indexed (however, only the X register can be used for indexing);
- The following diagrams show the operation of the shift and rotate instructions:

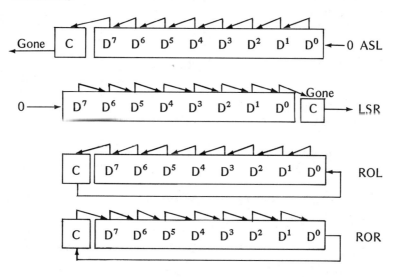

EXERCISES

1. What would be the decimal equivalent of the result of *shifting* the following binary number *two* times left?
   0 0 0 1 0 1 1 0 (binary number *before* shifts)
   _____ decimal equivalent *after two* shifts

Exercise 2 through 6 assume the following binary digits are in the accumulator and Processor Status Register. Show the contents of each after the specified instructions have been executed.

Accumulator | 0 | 1 | 0 | 1 | 0 | 0 | 1 | 1 | } at the beginning of *each* exercise

P register | 0 | 0 | 1 | 1 | 0 | 0 | 0 | 0 |
    N V   B D I Z C

2. After: ASL A   Accumulator | | | | | | | | |
       ASL A
       ASL A   P register | | 0 | 1 | 1 | 0 | 0 | |

3. After: LSR A   Accumulator | | | | | | | | |
       LSR A
                P register | | 0 | 1 | 1 | 0 | 0 | |

4. After: ROL A   Accumulator | | | | | | | | |
       ROL A
       ROL A   P register | | 0 | 1 | 1 | 0 | 0 | |

5. After: ROR A   Accumulator | | | | | | | | |
       ROR A
                P register | | 0 | 1 | 1 | 0 | 0 | |

6. After: ROR A   Accumulator | | | | | | | | |
       LSR A
       ROL A   P register | | 0 | 1 | 1 | 0 | 0 | |
       ASL A

7. Assume you are using the Right Shifter Program, and you use the following command sequence:

```
DEBUG
C1100< FF,08
G1000
```

(a) Show the bits contained in the accumulator at the end.

| | | | | | | | |

(b) the Carry bit is _____
                (set, reset)

8. In exercise 7, show the contents of these memory locations in hexadecimal notation.

1102	
1103	
1104	
1105	
1106	
1107	
1108	
1109	

ANSWERS

From Figure 10-7

A=00 X=0A Y=00 P=32

(a)

Address	Data
1100	91
1101	03
1102	18
1103	24
1104	12

(b)

Address	Data
1100	33
1101	04
1102	19
1103	0C
1104	06
1105	03

(c)

Address	Data
1100	E7
1101	06
1102	73
1103	39
1104	1C
1105	0E
1106	07
1107	03

1. 88 decimal (64+16+8)

2. Accumulator | 1 | 0 | 0 | 1 | 1 | 0 | 0 | 0 |

   P register | 1 | 0 | 1 | 1 | 0 | 0 | 0 | 0 | N=1, Z=0, C=0

3. Accumulator | 0 | 0 | 0 | 1 | 0 | 1 | 0 | 0 |

   P register | 0 | 0 | 1 | 1 | 0 | 0 | 0 | 1 | N=0, Z=0, C=1

4. Accumulator | 1 | 0 | 0 | 1 | 1 | 0 | 0 | 1 |

   P register | 1 | 0 | 1 | 1 | 0 | 0 | 0 | 0 | N=1, Z=0, C=0

5. Accumulator

1	0	0	1	0	1	0	0

P register

1	0	1	1	0	0	0	1

N=1, Z=0, C=1

6. Accumulator

0	1	0	1	0	0	1	0

P register

0	0	1	1	0	0	0	0

N=0, Z=0, C=0

7. (a)

0	0	0	0	0	0	0	0

   (b)   set

8.

1102	7F
1103	3F
1104	1F
1105	0F
1106	07
1107	03
1108	01
1109	00

Chapter 11

Multiplication, Division, and Subroutines

Since the 6502 instruction set does not contain instructions for multiplication and division, it is up to you to develop methods to perform these operations. Multiplication can be thought of as a series of additions.

Example:

$3 \times 12 = 12 + 12 + 12$
     and
$5 \times 16 = 16 + 16 + 16 + 16 + 16$

You can very easily write a program using a loop to add one number a specified number of times to obtain the same answer that would result from multiplying the two numbers.

```
          MULTIPLICATION BY ADDITION

          CLC
          LDX #5              Load X with one number
          LDA #0
LOOP ADC $1100               Add second number each
          DEX                    time through the loop
          BNE  LOOP
          END
```

If a second number (10 for example) is loaded into memory location 1100, and the program is assembled and executed, the accumulator would contain the desired result at the end of the program.

Although it is very quick and easy to write a program for this method, you can see that it would be time consuming to execute the multiplication of large numbers. That would require many passes through the loop. It would work for 8-bit numbers but would have to be redesigned for larger numbers requiring more than 8 bits. Due to the inefficiency of the program, it is seldom used.

Division could be performed in a similar manner, subtracting the divisor each time through a loop. However, that method has the same drawbacks of the multiplication method.

Since you've learned all about shifts and rotates in Chapter 10, let's see if you can make use of them to solve multiplication and division problems.

EIGHT-BIT MULTIPLICATION

Let's start with 8-bit numbers and look at the multiplication process first. Remember, the computer does its arithmetic using binary numbers. First look at a pencil-and-paper example of binary multiplication. Multiply 18 (decimal) by 58 (decimal) using both decimal and binary multiplication.

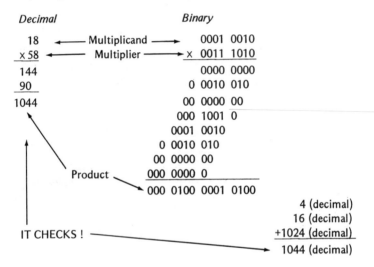

Notice that your multiplication involves adding the multiplicand every time that a one appears in the multiplier. Of course, there is a *shift* to the *left* each time a bit of the multiplier is used just as there is in decimal multiplication. You also proceed from right to left as you "use up" the bits of the multiplier.

The program that we will use does much the same thing. The first part of the program will initialize the memories with the appropriate values. We will store these quantities in memory as follows:

Memory Address	Contents
1100	Most Significant Byte of product
1101	Least Significant Byte of product
1102	Multiplicand (12)
1103	Multiplier (3A)

Figure 11-1. Memory Use for Multiplication

The accumulator will temporarily hold the Least Significant Byte of the product as the program is executed. You may notice that the multiplier is used from left to right (the opposite of the usual paper-and-pencil method) to simplify the process.

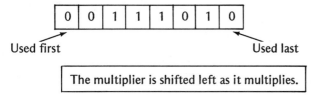

Used first   Used last

> The multiplier is shifted left as it multiplies.

The flowchart in Figure 11-2 clarifies the action in the program.

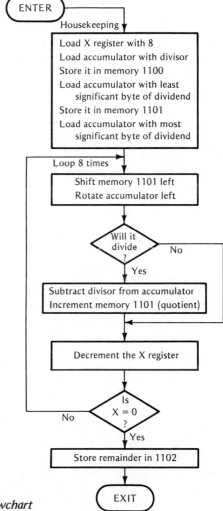

Figure 11-2. 8-bit Multiplication Flowchart

The housekeeping chores at the beginning of the program are easy for you now. You have used each instruction in this section of the program before. They are all either load or store instructions in various addressing modes.

This section of the assembly language program would look like this:

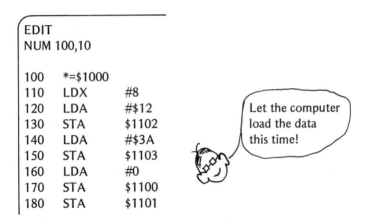

```
EDIT
NUM 100,10

100    *=$1000
110    LDX    #8
120    LDA    #$12
130    STA    $1102
140    LDA    #$3A
150    STA    $1103
160    LDA    #0
170    STA    $1100
180    STA    $1101
```

Let the computer load the data this time!

The loop section performs the multiplication. Two instructions appear that you learned about in the last chapter. One of them is ASL (Arithmetic Shift Left). It is used to shift the contents of the accumulator at statement number 190. It is also used in the Absolute Addressing mode at statement number 210. When used in this mode, the bits of the specified memory location (1103) are shifted left.

Example:

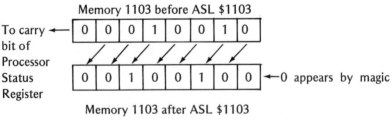

Memory 1103 before ASL $1103

To carry bit of Processor Status Register

| 0 | 0 | 0 | 1 | 0 | 0 | 1 | 0 |

| 0 | 0 | 1 | 0 | 0 | 1 | 0 | 0 | ←0 appears by magic

Memory 1103 after ASL $1103

We will make use of the fact that the Most Significant Bit from the shift is moved to the carry bit of the Processor Status Register.

At statement 200, you will make use of the ROL (Rotate Left) instruction in the Absolute Addressing mode. In Chapter 10, you used this instruction with the accumulator. This time it is used to rotate the bits in memory address 1100.

Example:

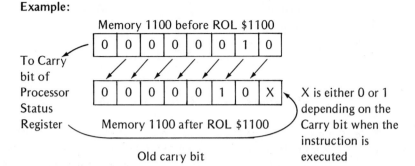

As each instruction is executed, the Most Significant Bit moves into the Carry bit of the Processor Status Register. In the ASL instruction, the Least Significant Bit is filled with a zero. In the ROL instruction, the Least Significant Bit is filled from the Carry bit of the status register (either a 1 or a 0). The instructions derive their names from the action that they cause.

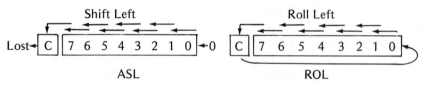

Here is the section that performs the loop, which is the heart of the program.

```
190  LOOP  ASL  A
200        ROL  $1100
210        ASL  $1103
220        BCC  SKIP
230        CLC
240        ADC  $1102
250        BCC  SKIP
260        INC  $1100
270  SKIP  DEX
280        BNE  LOOP
```

After the loop has been executed 8 times (once for each bit in the multiplier, the Least Significant Byte of the result will be in the accumulator. This is stored in the final section of the program in memory location 1101 for later display. The program then ends.

The Most Significant Byte of the result is now in memory location 1100, and the Least Significant Byte of the result is in memory location 1101.

The Last Section

```
290   STA   $1101
300   END
```

USING THE 8-BIT MULTIPLICATION PROGRAM

Enter the program in the Writer/Editor mode. Then assemble it. We used the Atari 820 Printer as we assembled the **Multiplication Program** so that we could see the complete program at one time. It is a long program, and it may not all show on the video screen. Here is what our printed assembled program looks like.

0000		0100	*=	$1000
1000	A208	0110	LDX	#8
1002	A912	0120	LDA	#$12
1004	8D0211	0130	STA	$1102
1007	A93A	0140	LDA	#$3A
1009	8D0311	0150	STA	$1103
100C	A900	0160	LDA	#0
100E	8D0011	0170	STA	$1100
1011	8D0111	0180	STA	$1101
1014	0A	0190 LOOP	ASL	A
1015	2E0011	0200	ROL	$1100
1018	0E0311	0210	ASL	$1103
101B	9009	0220	BCC	SKIP
101D	18	0230	CLC	
101E	6D0211	0240	ADC	$1102
1021	9003	0250	BCC	SKIP
1023	EE0011	0260	INC	$1100
1026	CA	0270 SKIP	DEX	
1027	D0EB	0280	BNE	LOOP
1029	8D0111	0290	STA	$1101
		0300 END		

Figure 11-3. Printout of Assembled Multiplication Program

You're ready to execute the program. You don't have to load any data this time as the program is going to do it for you. Enter the DEBUGGER and execute the program.

```
EDIT
BUG

DEBUG
G1000
102C            A=14 X=00 Y=00 P=32 S=00
DEBUG
■
```

The result of the multiplication can be found in memory locations 1100 (Most Significant Byte) and 1101 (Least Significant Byte). You can display them both at once by typing:

D1100,1101

```
.
.
DEBUG
D1100,1101

1100 04 14
DEBUG
■
```

Hmmm, let's see:
0414 hex =
0000010000010100 binary =
4+16+1024 = 1044 decimal.

It checks with our previously hand-calculated result.

While you are in the Debugger mode, make changes to the multiplier and multiplicand. They are in memory locations 1003 and 1008. Try using the following pairs of hexadecimal numbers and put your results in the appropriate places in Figure 11-4.

Multiplier (1003)	Multiplicand (1008)	Result (1100 and 1010)
03	09	
1A	E4	
3C	D8	
A4	C2	
FF	FF	

Figure 11-4. Multiplication Exercises

Remember, there is a Change Memory command in the Debugger mode. Here are two ways to get ready for the first modification.

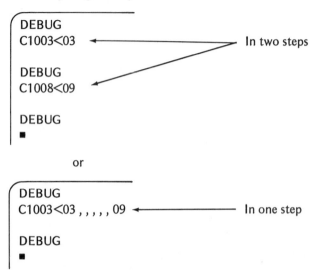

```
DEBUG
C1003<03                                    In two steps

DEBUG
C1008<09

DEBUG
■
```

or

```
DEBUG
C1003<03 , , , , , 09                       In one step

DEBUG
■
```

Most people working with machine language programming agree that an assembler removes much of the drudgery. If the previous multiplication program had been programmed in machine language directly, there would have been many details to take care of.

- Individual addresses would have had to be assigned to each instruction and its operand.
- Branch locations would have had to be calculated.
- Individual Op Codes would have had to be looked up in an instruction table.
- Conversion between decimal and hexadecimal notation would have been necessary.

The Atari Assembler programs make life much easier. The **Writer/Editor Program** cannot execute a program directly, but it takes care of assigning Op Codes and the operands that go into the machine language **Object Program**.

The Assembler relies on the **Debugger Program** for execution of the assembled program and for examination of memory for results. The combination of Editor, Assembler, and Debugger are hard to beat. The Assembler does all the detail work, and the Debugger provides the execution and debugging capabilities. Of course, the Editor allows you to communicate your wishes to the Assembler.

After that brief introduction to multiplication, let's move on and take a look at the division process.

EIGHT-BIT DIVISION

Once again, we'll take a look at pencil-and-paper division before looking at the computer's method. Since division is the inverse operation of multiplication, we'll use the same numbers that we used in the multiplication example with one exception. That exception is made to the dividend so that the division example will not come out even. There will be a remainder.

Example:

$$1046 \text{ (decimal)} \quad \div \quad 58 \text{ (decimal)}$$

Decimal   Binary

```
        18 quotient                                    1  0010 quotient
   58 )1046                        0011 1010 ) 0100 0001 0110
        58                                     0011 1010
       466                                        111 011
       464                                        111 010
         2 remainder                                  10 remainder
```

It checks ───────────→ { 1 0010 = 12 HEX = 18 dec.
                          10 = 2 HEX = 2 dec.

Just as in multiplication, you can see shifts being made as the division takes place. Place value is very important in this process. Notice that a subtraction is made only if the divisor is smaller than part of the dividend that is being tested. A one then is placed in the quotient. If the divisor is larger, a zero is placed in the quotient.

Our assembly language program for division will look much the same as the multiplication program. The first part of the program places the appropriate values in their respective memory locations. Figure 11-5 shows the placement of the data.

Memory Address	*Contents*	
	At the Start	*At the End*
Accumulator	Most Significant Byte of dividend	Remainder
1100	Divisor	Quotient
1101	Least Significant Byte of dividend	—
1102	—	Remainder

Figure 11-5. Memory Use for Division

The flowchart for the program is given in Figure 11-6. The accumulator and memory location 1101 begin with the original dividend. Each time through the loop, the contents of memory location 1101 are shifted left, and the accumulator is rotated left. If a carry occurs from the shift of memory location 1101, it will appear as a 1 in the Least Significant Bit of the accumulator when it is rotated. If no carry occurs from the memory 1101 shift, a zero appears in the Least Significant Bit of the accumulator. Thus each time through the loop, the dividend is shifted one place from memory 1101 to the accumulator. This lets the computer compare the divisor with the most significant part of the dividend for a trial division.

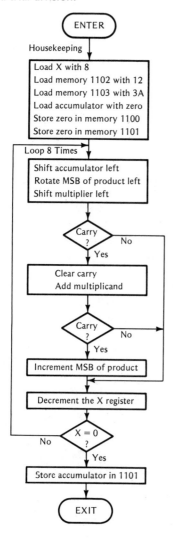

Figure 11-6. Division Flowchart

The division is accomplished by comparing the divisor with the accumulator. Every time that the divisor is smaller than, or equal to, the accumulator, the divisor is subtracted from the accumulator and memory 1101 is incremented by one. This means a 1 is appearing in the quotient.

If the divisor is larger than the accumulator, no subtraction is made and memory 1101 is not incremented. This means a zero appears in the quotient.

As the bits in the accumulator and memory 1101 move to the left, the quotient appears in memory 1101 from the right (0 if divisor did not go into dividend, 1 if divisor did go into dividend).

After the loop is completed (8 passes through), the remainder is placed in memory location 1102. When the program is complete, you'll find the 8-bit quotient in memory location 1101 and the remainder in memory location 1102.

The housekeeping chores are similar to those of the **Multiplication Program.**

```
10    *=$1000
20    LDX   #8
30    LDA   #$3A
40    STA   $1100
50    LDA   #$16
60    STA   $1101
70    LDA   #4
```

The main part of the program comes next. The rotate instruction appears in a different form in the loop in this program. We are using ROL A to rotate the accumulator. It works the same way as it did when we rotated a memory location. Only this time, the accumulator's contents are rotated. The loop is again executed 8 times using the X register as a counter.

```
80    LOOP  ASL $1101
90          ROL A
100         CMP $1100
110         BCC BRANCH
120         SBC $1100
130         INC $1101
140   BRANCH DEX
150         BNE LOOP
```

When the loop has been completed 8 times, the contents of the accumulator (the remainder) is stored in memory location 1102 for ease of display.

```
160   STA   $1102
170   END
```

Enter and assemble the program now. The assembled program should look like this:

```
0000                    10          *=      $1000
1000    A208            20          LDX     #8
1002    A93A            30          LDA     #$3A
1004    8D0011          40          STA     $1100
1007    A916            50          LDA     #$16
1009    8D0111          60          STA     $1101
100C    A904            70          LDA     #4
100E    0E0111          80 LOOP     ASL     $1101
1011    2A              90          ROL     A
1012    CD0011          0100        CMP     $1100
1015    9006            0110        BCC     BRANCH
1017    ED0011          0120        SBC     $1100
101A    EE0111          0130        INC     $1101
101D    CA              0140 BRANCH DEX
101E    D0EE            0150        BNE     LOOP
1020    8D0211          0160        STA     $1102
                        0170 END
```

Figure 11-7. Printout of Assembled Division Program

Enter the Debugger mode, execute the program, and display the results.

```
EDIT
BUG

DEBUG
G1000
1023        A=22 X=00 Y=00 P=32 S=00
DEBUG
D1101,1102
                            ──── Quotient
1101 12 02
                            ──── Remainder
DEBUG
■
```

This checks with the hand calculated result.

Try the additional division problems given in Figure 11-8. The answers appear at the end of the chapter exercises.

Dividend		Divisor	Result	
MSB (100D)	LSB (1008)	(1003)	Quotient (1101)	Remainder (1102)
01	00	10		
0A	BC	DE		
0A	05	9F		
05	AA	83		
7F	FF	FF		

Figure 11-8. Division Exercises

If you try any other examples, make sure that the quotients do not exceed FF. The program *will not work* for quotients larger than one byte.

SUBROUTINES

Quite often, a set of instructions must be executed at several different places within a program. Rather than write the instructions at each place they are used in the program, it is more efficient to write the instructions once, as a subroutine to your program. Each time that you wish to execute the set of instructions, you insert the Jump to SubRoutine instruction.

Example:

Suppose that you have a subroutine labeled SUBEEP. The JSR instruction would be:

JSR SUBEEP

Once you have executed the subroutine, you must have a way to get back to the main program. And you must come back to the instruction that follows the JSR instruction that sent you to the subroutine. This is done by placing a RTS (ReTurn from Subroutine) instruction as the last instruction executed in the subroutine.

Subroutine
Instructions

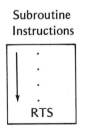

RTS

The subroutine could be "called" from the main program by the JSR SUBEEP instruction. The subroutine would be executed, and control would be returned to the main program as follows:

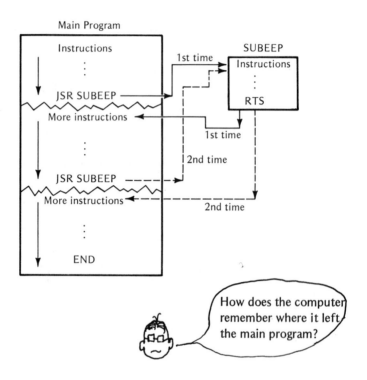

Figure 11-9. Subroutine Flow

Remember the stack that was discussed in Chapters 1 and 5? When a JSR instruction is executed, the computer automatically places the memory address contained in the program counter on the stack. Then, when the RTS instruction is executed at the end of the subroutine, the computer takes the address from the stack and places it back in the program counter. The execution of the main program then continues from that point.

Jumping to the Subroutine

.
.
.
.
.

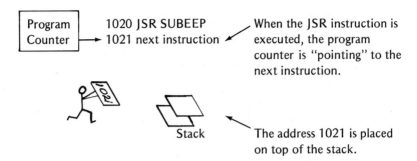

Program Counter | 1020 JSR SUBEEP
1021 next instruction

When the JSR instruction is executed, the program counter is "pointing" to the next instruction.

Stack

The address 1021 is placed on top of the stack.

The address of the subroutine is placed in the program counter.

1100 021   Program Counter

The program counter then forces the computer to execute the instructions beginning at location 1100 (the subroutine).

Returning from the Subroutine

The subroutine is executed

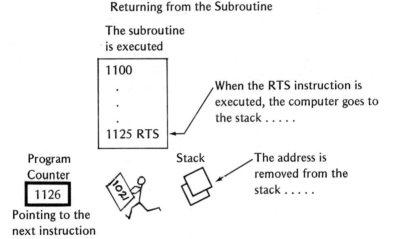

1100
.
.
.
1125 RTS

When the RTS instruction is executed, the computer goes to the stack . . . . .

Program Counter

1126

Pointing to the next instruction

Stack

The address is removed from the stack . . . . .

Program Counter

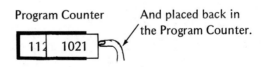

11 1021

And placed back in the Program Counter.

This forces the computer to execute the next instruction starting at location 1021.

You should remember that the stack is made up of 8-bit memory locations. Addresses may be 16 bits long. Therefore, the process is a little more complicated than the previous description indicates. The address is actually placed on the stack as two separate bytes.

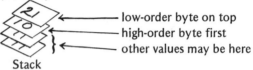

Stack

low-order byte on top
high-order byte first
other values may be here

When the RTS instruction is executed, the return address is also picked off the stack in two separate bytes. In other words, the RTS instruction reverses the process performed by the JSR instruction. They work together just like the GO-SUB and RETURN instructions of BASIC.

Subroutines in assembly language may be nested, just as subroutines in BASIC.

USING A SUBROUTINE

Let's return to the 8-bit multiplication program used earlier in this chapter and add a sound subroutine that will play a different sound each time one of the bits of the multiplier is used. You will need to insert many new instructions in the original program. Several new instructions will be introduced which use the stack to save and retrieve information.

THE MAIN PROGRAM (Unchanged Portion)

```
100    *=$100
110    LDX    #8          ⎫
120    LDA    #$12        ⎪
130    STA    $1102       ⎪  Data Initialization
140    LDA    #$3A        ⎬
150    STA    $1103       ⎪
160    LDA    #0          ⎪
170    STA    $1100       ⎪
180    STA    $1101       ⎭
190    LOOP   ASL  A      ⎫
200    ROL    $1100       ⎪
210    ASL    $1103       ⎪  Multiplication Loop
220    BCC    SKIP        ⎬
230    CLC                ⎪
240    ADC    $1102       ⎪
250    BCC    SKIP        ⎪
260    INC    $1100       ⎭
```

MAIN PROGRAM (Changed Portion)

```
270  SKIP PHA
280       PHP
290       TXA
300       PHA
310       JSR SUBEEP  ◄──── Here's where you GOSUB
320       PLA  ◄──────────── You come back here
330       TAX
340       PLP
350       PLA
360       DEX
370       BNE LOOP
380       STA $1101
390       BRK  ◄──────── Program ends here
```

Subroutine SUBEEP

```
              400  SUBEEP LDA #$C8
  1024        410       STA $CE
              420       LDA #A0
              430       STA $D201
              440       LDA $1103,X
              450       STA $D200
  SUBEEP      460       LDA #$AF
              470  ALOOP STA $D201
              480       LDA $CE
              490       JSR DELAY   ◄────── Jump to nested sub
  1051        500       SEC         ◄────── Return here
              510       SBC #$01
              520       CMP #$9F
              530       BNE ALOOP
              540       RTS         ◄────── End of SUBEEP
  1059        550  DELAY LDY #$13   ◄────── Start of nested sub
              560  DELAY2 DEY
  Nested      570       BNE DELAY2
  Subroutine  580       DEX
              590       BNE DELAY
              600       RTS         ◄────── End of Nested sub
  1061        610  END
```

The program is executed in the order shown in Figure 11-10. The subroutine SUBEEP is called eight times from the main program. The subroutine labeled DELAY is nested within subroutine SUBEEP.

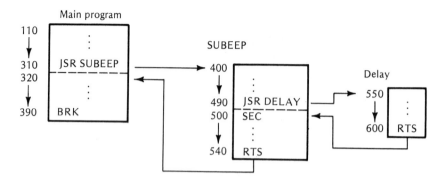

Figure 11-10. Sound Subroutine Flow

The frequency of the sound is controlled by the value stored in D200 from the data table at 1103+X. The audio control register at D201 controls the volume of the sound.

Since the 6502 microprocessor has only two index registers (X and Y), a new programming technique is demonstrated at 270–300 and 320–350. The main program *and* the subroutines use the X register and accumulator for different purposes. Therefore, *before* the subroutines are called, all the values in registers X, A, and P are saved on the stack so that the registers may be used by the subroutines in their own way.

PHA PusH the Accumulator on the stack
PHP PusH the P register on the stack
TXA and PHA Transfer X to Z, then PusH A on the stack

When JSR is executed, the information goes on the stack in this way.

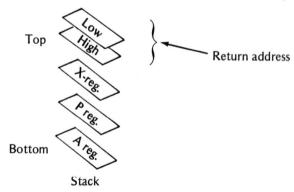

When SUBEEP's RTS instruction is executed, the return address is pulled off the stack leaving the following data.

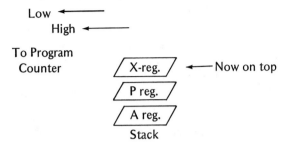

The computer then returns to the main program and executes in order:

PLA ⎫ ⟵ Pull off top of stack and
TAX ⎭   transfer to X register

PLP ⟵ Pull off stack and place in P register

PLA ⟵ Pull off stack and place in A register

Notice that values are pulled off the stack in the reverse order of the way they were pushed on. This restores everything to the proper place.

Enter the program as given and assemble it. Then go to DEBUG and enter the data in the data table at 1104 through 110B.

Address	Data
1104	48
1105	60
1106	78
1107	90
1108	A8
1109	C0
110A	D8
110B	F0

Figure 11-11. Data for Sound Program

Execute the program and see how you like the notes that are produced by the sound subroutine SUBEEP. If you want to change the notes, change the data shown in Figure 11-11. The frequencies are picked off in reverse order from 110B through 1104.

SUMMARY

You have now seen how two operations for which the computer has no instructions can be performed by putting together groups of other instructions. Although the 6502 microprocessor has no multiplication or division instructions, the operations can be performed as a series of additions, subtractions, and shifts or rotations. You have learned in this chapter to:

- Apply the shift and rotate instructions in programs to multiply and divide numbers;
- Use a demonstration program that multiplies two 8-bit numbers to produce a 16-bit result;
- Use a demonstration program that divides an 8-bit divisor into a 16-bit dividend producing an 8-bit quotient and an 8-bit remainder;
- Use a subroutine called by a JSR (Jump to SubRoutine) instruction and return to the main program with a RTS (ReTurn from Subroutine) instruction;
- Use the stack to save and retrieve information when registers or counters must be used in more than one way;
- Use the following other new instructions;
  PHA   Push the value in the accumulator onto the stack
  PHP   Push the P register's contents onto the stack
  PLA   Pull the top value off the stack and put it into the accumulator
  PLP   Pull the top value off the stack and put it into the P register
- Use a subroutine producing musical tones

EXERCISES

1. Multiply the decimal numbers 28 and 37.
   (a) Using decimal notation

   ```
   28
   x 37
   ```

   (b) Using binary notation

   ```
   28=
   x 37= _____
   ```

   (c) Check the binary result

   ```
      _____
   +  _____
   +  _____
   ```

2. According to the flowchart in Figure 11-2, which bit of the multiplier is used first? _____

(most significant, least significant)

Exercises 3–7 refer to the following sketches of the Carry bit and the accumulator before and after one of the shift or rotate instructions are given.

(a) Carry   Accumulator

| 1 | | 01010111 | before |
| 0 | | 10101110 | after |

(c) Carry   Accumulator

| 1 | | 01010111 | before |
| 1 | | 00101011 | after |

(b) Carry   Accumulator

| 1 | | 01010111 | before |
| 0 | | 10101111 | after |

(d) Carry   Accumulator

| 1 | | 01010111 | before |
| 1 | | 10101011 | after |

3. Name the shift or rotate instruction performed in a. _____

4. Name the shift or rotate instruction performed in b. _____

5. Name the shift or rotate instruction performed in c. _____

6. Name the shift or rotate instruction performed in d. _____

7. Fill in the blanks which would result from successive operations for your answers from Exercises 3, 4, 5, and 6.

Originally: Carry   Accumulator

| 1 | | 01010111 |

The instructions for your answers to:
    3, then 4, then 5, then 6 are executed.

Final conditions:

Carry   Accumulator

| | | |

8. The 8-bit multiplication program of Figure 11-3 is to be used to multiply 120 (decimal) by 73 (decimal).
   (a) What hexadecimal values must be loaded into which two memory locations?

Address	Data

(b) Show how to use the DEBUGGER to load the values by one command.

```
·
·
DEBUG
```

9. The assembly language instruction used to call a subroutine labeled SUBBY would be:

_____   _____

10. The last instruction executed by a subroutine must be: _____

ANSWERS

Answers to Figure 11-4

Multiplier	Multiplicand	Result
03	09	00 1B
1A	E4	17 28
3C	D8	32 A0
A4	C2	7C 48
FF	FF	FE 01

Answers to Figure 11-8

Dividend	Divisor	Result	
		Quotient	Remainder
01 00	10	10	00
0A BC	DE	0C	54
0A 05	9F	10	15
05 AA	83	0B	09
7F FF	FF	80	7F

1. (a) Using decimal notation

```
    28
  × 37
   196
    84
  1036
```

(b) Using binary notation

18=	00011100
× 37=	00100101
	00011100
	00000000
	00011100
	00000000
	00000000
	00011100
	0010000001100

(c)

4
+8
+1024
1036

2. Most Significant Bit

3. ASL A

4. ROL A

5. LSR A

6. ROR A

7. Final conditions:

Carry   Accumulator

0	00010111

8. (a)

Address	Data
1003	49
1008	78

the data could be reversed

(b)

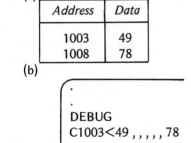

```
        .
        .
     DEBUG
     C1003<49 , , , , , 78
```

9. JSR SUBBY

10. RTS

Chapter 12

Programming Practice

Much can be learned about programming by using, analyzing, and modifying programs written by other people. By this time, you are familiar with the use of the Atari Assembler Cartridge and should feel at ease using it. Therefore, we have devoted this last chapter to programs for you to use and modify to fit your own needs. Suggestions are given for some modifications, and you will no doubt think of others.

We have not covered all of the features of the Assembler Cartridge but have tried to present those that we think you will use most.

Programming requires much practice. Therefore, you should try other programs to investigate all aspects of the 6502 instruction set, as well as Atari Assembler Cartridge commands and statements. Seek out those instructions that you are not familiar with, study the descriptions, and write some short simple programs that make use of them.

The assembler can be used to develop machine language subroutines that can speed up and make your BASIC programs more powerful. Many applications using sound effects, high speed graphics, animation, and certain functions not available in BASIC can be performed by machine language subroutines.

As we cautioned earlier, your machine language programs require their own area of memory. If you are using assembled subroutines accessed from BASIC, you must be careful that your machine language programs are assembled in an area of memory that is not used by the BASIC program. There is an area of memory from 0600 (1536 decimal) through 06FF (1791 decimal) that can be used for this purpose. These 256 bytes that are available will be adequate for most of your machine language subroutines. All programs in this chapter use this area. There are also 7 bytes of zero page memory that have been reserved for your use by the BASIC cartridge (locations CB through D1 or 203 decimal, through 209, decimal). In addition, locations D4 and D5 of zero page are used to return parameters (numerical values) from machine language subroutines to BASIC through the USR function.

The Assembler User's Manual, supplied with your Assembler Cartridge, contains several entertaining programs. The manual also shows a method to prepare an assembled subroutine and a BASIC program which will access the subroutine. We will concentrate in this chapter on similar programs that use only the Assembler Cartridge. You may rewrite them to be accessed from BASIC if you wish. Our first program will demonstrate both methods of using the assembled program.

BASIC language can perform logic functions by means of the statements NOT, AND and OR. There is another logic function in the 6502 instruction set, the Exclusive OR. Our first program demonstrates its use.

USING A LOGIC FUNCTION

The 6502 microprocessor has instructions that extend the logic functions NOT, AND and OR used in BASIC. One of these instructions performs the logic function Exclusive OR (Assembly mnemonic EOR). This instruction compares two binary numbers, one bit position at a time. If the two bits are alike, a zero is placed in the corresponding bit position of the result. If one of the compared bits is a 1 (one) and the other is a 0 (zero), a 1 (one) is placed in the corresponding bit position of the result.

Example:

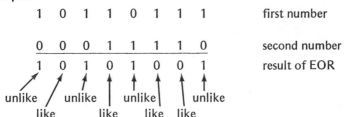

1	0	1	1	0	1	1	1	first number
0	0	0	1	1	1	1	0	second number
1	0	1	0	1	0	0	1	result of EOR

You see that a 1 results in a given bit position if there is a one in the corresponding bit position of *either* one number *or* the other number, *but not* if there is a one in the corresponding bit position of *both* numbers.

The above example shows that the result of performing an Exclusive OR on the hex numbers B7 and 1E is A9.

Let's now write an assembly language program to perform the same Exclusive OR as the example.

EOR SOURCE PROGRAM

```
100    *=$0600          start program at 0600
110    LDA   #$B7
120    EOR   #$1E        EOR B7 and 1E
130    STA   $1000
140    END
```

Enter and assemble the program.

ASSEMBLED DISPLAY

```
.
.
.
130    STA      $1000
140    END
ASM
0000                    100       *=      $0600

0600   A9B7             110       LDA    #$B7

0602   491E             120       EOR    #$1E

0604   8D0010           130       STA    $1000

                        140  END

EDIT
■
```

Enter the DEBUGGER and execute the program

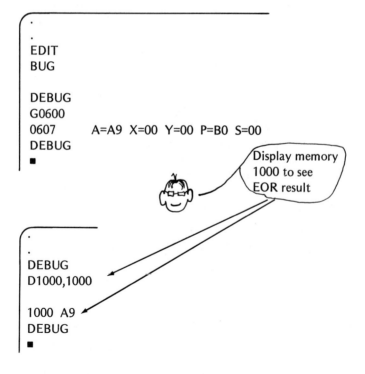

```
.
.
.
EDIT
BUG

DEBUG
G0600
0607      A=A9  X=00  Y=00  P=B0  S=00
DEBUG
■
```

Display memory
1000 to see
EOR result

```
.
.
.
DEBUG
D1000,1000

1000 A9
DEBUG
■
```

There it is, very short and quick. Now let's see how we might access a similar subroutine from BASIC. The values to be Exclusive ORed will be passed from the BASIC subroutine to the subroutine. The subroutine will pull the values off the stack, EOR them and pass the result back to BASIC. The flow of the program and subroutine is shown in Figure 12-1.

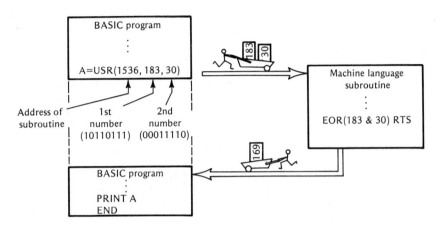

Figure 12-1. Logic Program Flowchart

The BASIC program is very short. Do not enter it in the computer yet. Remember the procedure mentioned earlier.

```
100    REM ** EOR SUBROUTINE PROGRAM **
110    GR.0
120    A = USR(1536,183,30)
130    PRINT "183 EXCLUSIVE OR WITH 30 IS":A
140    END
```

Notice the USR function at line 120. The data in parentheses following the address 1536 is placed on the stack for use by the subroutine in this order:

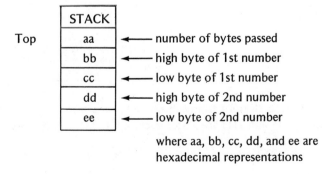

where aa, bb, cc, dd, and ee are hexadecimal representations

The machine language subroutine will pull the top byte off the stack. It is not used. The high byte of the 1st number is then pulled off and saved (in memory $CC). Then the low byte of the 1st number is pulled off and saved (in memory $CD). You now have this condition:

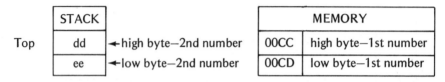

	STACK	
Top	dd	◄─high byte—2nd number
	ee	◄─low byte—2nd number

MEMORY	
00CC	high byte—1st number
00CD	low byte—1st number

The subroutine then pulls off the high byte of the second number (from the stack) and Exclusive ORs it with the high byte of the first number (from memory $CC). The result is stored in memory $D5. You now have:

	STACK	
Top	ee	low byte—2nd number

MEMORY	
00CC	high byte—1st number
00CD	low byte—1st number
.	.
.	.
.	.
00D5	high byte—result

Next, the subroutine pulls off the low byte of the second number (from the stack) and Exclusive ORs it with the low byte of the first number (from memory $CD). The result is stored in memory $D4. You now have:

	STACK	
Top	??	all variables passed by USR are gone

MEMORY	
00CC	high byte—1st number
00CD	low byte—1st number
.	.
.	.
.	.
00D4	low byte—result
00D5	high byte—result

Last of all, the RTS (Return from subroutine) instruction is executed. The values stored in $D5 and $D4 are passed back to the BASIC program as the decimal value for the variable A.

This is what the machine language subroutine looks like:

```
100        *=$0600
110    EXOR PLA        ◄── number of data bytes
120    PLA             ◄── get high byte—1st number
130    STA $CC         ◄── and store
140    PLA        }
150    STA $CD    }    ◄── now the low byte
160    PLA             ◄── high byte—2nd number
170    EOR $CC         ◄── exclusive or
180    STA $D5         ◄── and store
190    PLA        }        now the low bytes
200    EOR $CD    }    ◄──
210    STA $D4    }
220    RTS             ◄── now return
230    END
```

ENTERING THE SUBROUTINE

Now, go through the steps outlined in the
Assembler User's Manual.

1. Place the Assembler Cartridge in the computer and
enter the assembly language subroutine.

2. Assemble the program to make sure that you have
no errors.

```
EDIT
ASM

0000            0100        *=    $0600
0600   68       0110   EXOR PLA
0601   68       0120        PLA
0602   85CC     0130        STA   $CC
0604   68       0140        PLA
0605   85CD     0150        STA   $CD
0607   68       0160        PLA
0608   45CC     0170        EOR   $CC
060A   85D5     0180        STA   $D5
060C   68       0190        PLA
060D   45CD     0200        EOR   $CD
060F   85D4     0210        STA   $D4
0611   60       0220        RTS
                0230   END

EDIT
■
```

3. Use 3(a) for cassette storage or 3(b) for disk storage and assemble again.

(a) For cassette:

```
.
.
EDIT
ASM,,#C:
```
Press RETURN
After the "BEEP" press RETURN AGAIN

(b) For disk:

```
ASM,,#D:EXOR.OBJ
```
Press RETURN

4. Take out the Assembler Cartridge and replace it with the BASIC cartridge.
5. Wait for the BASIC READY prompt.

```
.
READY
■
```

6. Use 6(a) for cassette or 6(b) for disk.

(a) Follow the normal procedure for loading from tape with:

```
CLOAD
```
and press RETURN

(b) Type in DOS to raise the Disk Operating System.

```
DISK OPERATING SYSTEM                        9/24/79
COPYRIGHT 1979 ATARI

A. DISK DIRECTORY          I. FORMAT DISK
B. RUN CARTRIDGE           J. DUPLICATE DISK
C. COPY FILE               K. BINARY SAVE
D. DELETE FILE(S)          L. BINARY LOAD
E. RENAME FILE             M. RUN AT ADDRESS
F. LOCK FILE               N. DEFINE DEVICE
G. UNLOCK FILE             O. DUPLICATE FILE
H. WRITE DOS FILE

SELECT ITEM
■
```

Then type L to load a binary file.

```
.
.
.
SELECT ITEM
L
LOAD FROM WHAT FILE?
■
```

Now, type: EXOR.OBJ   and press RETURN

```
.
.
SELECT ITEM
L
LOAD FROM WHAT FILE?
EXOR.OBJ
```

After the file is loaded, the computer will return to the SELECT ITEM PROMPT.

```
.
.
.
SELECT ITEM
■
```

Type B and press return to return to BASIC.

```
.
.
.
SELECT ITEM
B

READY
■
```

7. You should now be back in the BASIC READY mode.

8. Enter the BASIC program.

```
100   REM ** EOR SUBROUTINE PROGRAM **
110   CLS
120   A = USR(1536,183,30)
130   PRINT "183 EXCLUSIVE OR WITH 30 IS";A
140   END
■
```

You are now ready to execute your program—ALMOST. First check to make sure the machine language subroutine is in memory. This can be done by checking the first location of the subroutine. Type:

PRINT PEEK(1536) and press RETURN

The computer should respond with the value 104 (the decimal equivalent of the first machine language instruction, PLA).

If the computer responds correctly, execute the program with the RUN command. If it doesn't correspond correctly, go back to the Assembler Cartridge and try it all again. Verrrrry carefully.

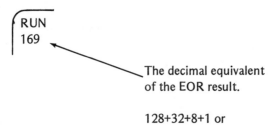

```
RUN
169
```

The decimal equivalent
of the EOR result.

128+32+8+1 or

10101001 in binary

You may use the Exclusive OR with other values by changing line 120 of the BASIC program.

120 A = USR(1536,183,30)

These values may change.

Do not change the value 1536 as that is the memory location where the subroutine begins. The other two values (183 and 30) may be changed to any positive integer in the range of 0 through 65535.

The remaining programs in this chapter will show only the versions of the programs that may be run directly in the Debugger mode of the assembler. Feel free to change them to subroutines to be accessed from BASIC as in the EOR program.

PROGRAM TO SOUND OFF

This program uses three sound registers (or channels) for playing music chords. The data is placed in the appropriate registers, and the sound produced is sent to your TV set. Be sure that you have the volume of your TV set turned to a reasonable level before running the program. The program controls the volume produced, but the TV volume control must be set high enough to make an audible sound.

The last chord produced will keep playing until a new note is placed in the sound registers. Therefore, the last part of the program sets the volume down to zero. There are other ways to accomplish the same result, but why not let the computer do it for you?

We have used comments in the source program that label each part of the program and the data values used. It is good programming practice to do so. If you save the source program on tape or disk, the comments will help you decipher the program when you enter it again. The flow of the program is shown in Figure 12-2.

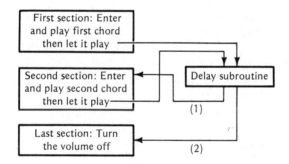

Figure 12-2. Sound Off Program Flow

SOUND OFF SOURCE PROGRAM

```
100    *=$0600
110    ;FIRST CHORD SECTION
120    LDA    #$79            FIRST NOTE
130    STA    $D200
140    LDA    #$88            SECOND NOTE
150    STA    $D202
160    LDA    #$99            THIRD NOTE
170    STA    $D204
180    LDA    #$AF            TONE AND VOLUME
190    STA    $D201
```

```
200    STA    $D203
210    STA    $D205
220    JSR    DELAY           PLAY AWHILE
230    ;SECOND CHORD SECTION
240    LDA    #$C1            FIRST NOTE
250    STA    $D200
260    LDA    #$D9            SECOND NOTE
270    STA    $D202
280    LDA    #$F3            THIRD NOTE
290    STA    $D204
300    LDA    #$A8            TONE AND VOLUME
310    STA    $D201
320    STA    $D203
330    STA    $D205
340    JSR    DELAY           PLAY AWHILE
350    ;TURN VOLUME OFF SECTION
360    LDA    #$A0
370    STA    $D201
380    STA    $D203
390    STA    $D205
400    BRK                    END OF MAIN PROGRAM
410    DELAY LDX #$FF
420    LOOP   LDY #$FF
430    LOOP1 DEY
440    BNE    LOOP1
450    DEX
460    BNE    LOOP
470    RTS
480    END                    END  OF  SOURCE  PROGRAM
```

Enter the program, assemble it, and execute it in the usual way. See if you like the sounds produced. If not, take a look at the table of music notes in Figure 12-3. You may alter frequency values in the program as long as you stay in the range of 0 (highest note) to FF hexadecimal (lowest note).

To understand the tone and volume controls, you must look at the volume in binary form.

Example:

195 decimal = AF hexadecimal

= 1010 1111

A   F ◄——————— highest volume

selects pure tone (no noise)

Natural Scale Note	Frequency Value (hex)	
C	1D	High
B	1F	
A#	21	
A	23	
G#	25	
G	28	
F#	2A	
F	2D	
E	2F	
D#	32	
D	35	
C#	39	
C	3C	
B	40	
A#	44	
A	48	
G#	4C	
G	51	
F#	55	
F	5B	
E	60	
D#	66	
D	6C	
C#	72	
C	79	Middle
B	80	
A#	88	
A	90	
G#	99	
G	A2	
F#	AC	
F	B6	
E	C1	
D#	CC	
D	D9	
C#	E6	
C	F3	Low

Figure 12-3. Approximate Values for Three-Octave Scale

The first hex digit (A in example) controls the noise content of the tone. We chose a pure tone. The second hex digit controls the volume. Its range may be from 0 (lowest volume = off) to F (highest volume).

You should try different values to obtain different sound effects. All you need to do is change the values for frequency, tone and volume. Check the comments in the source program to find the values to be changed.

1. Changes may be made in the source program.

    (a) In the Edit mode change lines:
       120, 140, 160, 180 for the first chord
       240, 260, 280, and 300 for second chord

    (b) Assemble the program again.

    (c) Execute it from the Debugger mode.

2. Changes may be made in the object program.
Use the Debugger mode to change memories:
    0601, 0606, 060B and 0610 for first chord
    061E, 0623, 0628 and 062D for second chord

PLAY NOTES PROGRAM

This program uses a single sound channel to play a series of notes. A time delay is used between the notes so that they can be heard for a reasonable length of time. Once again, make sure that the volume on the TV set is turned up. By looking at the frequency table of Figure 12-3, you can see that the program plays one octave of the scale.

ASSEMBLER PROGRAM

```
100    *=$0600
110    ;PLAY NOTES
120    LDA     #$AF          ◄────────Volume
130    STA     $D201
140    LDA     #$F3          ◄────────Freq. 1st note
150    JSR     RPT
160    LDA     #$D9          ◄────────Freq. 2nd note
170    JSR     RPT
180    LDA     #$C1          ◄────────Freq. 3rd note
190    JSR     RPT
200    LDA     #$B6                    etc.
210    JSR     RPT
220    LDA     #$A2
230    JSR     RPT
```

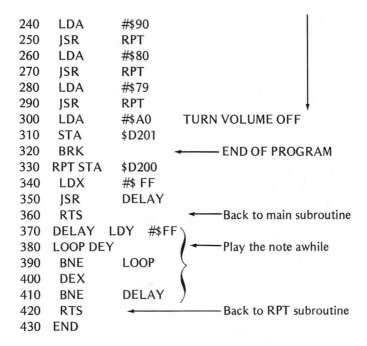

```
240   LDA       #$90
250   JSR       RPT
260   LDA       #$80
270   JSR       RPT
280   LDA       #$79
290   JSR       RPT
300   LDA       #$A0        TURN VOLUME OFF
310   STA       $D201
320   BRK                 ◄──────── END OF PROGRAM
330   RPT STA   $D200
340   LDX       #$ FF
350   JSR       DELAY
360   RTS                 ◄──────Back to main subroutine
370   DELAY  LDY   #$FF
380   LOOP DEY             ◄──────Play the note awhile
390   BNE       LOOP
400   DEX
410   BNE       DELAY
420   RTS       ◄──────────────── Back to RPT subroutine
430   END
```

Enter the program and assemble and execute it. Does it sound reasonable to you? If not, changes can be made where the frequencies are loaded into the accumulator. The duration of the notes can be changed by the LDY and LDX instructions in the RPT subroutine.

This program could be changed so that it would access the frequencies from a data table. The frequencies could then be accessed by an indexed load instruction. This might be a little difficult since the X and Y registers are already being used in the time delay subroutine. You would have to save their values on the stack, and retrieve them after the time delay had been completed. We have covered the use of the stack instructions before. Therefore, you know how to make these changes if you wish.

Notice in line 300 and 310 that the value A0 was stored in memory location D201. This sets the volume to zero. If those two lines were omitted, the last note would keep playing even though the program had ended.

PROGRAM TO SHAPE SOUND

This program uses one sound channel to shape the sound that is produced. If you look at a graph of the volume of the sound produced over a period of time, it would look something like this:

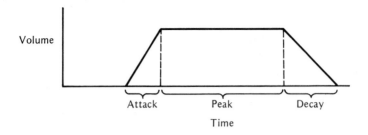

You can see that the sound goes through three distinct periods. You have used the frequency, tone and volume variables before. Now, you have a chance actually to vary the shape of the sound produced.

We have chosen one of the three time constants—the decay time. It will be changed as the program is executed. It is varied from 50 to 200 (decimal) within a loop in steps of 25 (50, 75, 100, 125, 150, 175 and 200). The sound is thus shaped as follows:

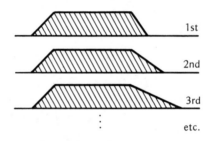

SOUND SHAPER PROGRAM

```
100    *=$0600
110    ;INITIALIZE TIMES
120    LDA   #$3C      FREQUENCY
130    STA   $D200
140    LDA   #$32      PEAK
150    STA   $CD
160    LDA   #$0A      ATTACK
170    STA   $CC
180    LOOP  LDA $1000      COUNTER
190    TAX
200    LDA   $1000,X
210    STA   $CE      DECAY
220    DEC   $1000
230    LDA   #$A0      VOLUME
240    ATTK  STA $D201
250    LDX   $CC
260    JSR   DELAY
270    CLC
```

```
280     ADC   #$01
290     CMP   #$80
300     BNE   ATTK
310     LDA   #$0E
320 PEAK   LDX $CD
330     JSR   DELAY
340     SEC
350     SBC   #$01
360     BNE   PEAK
370     LDA   #$AF        TONE,VOLUME
380 DCAY   STA $D201
390     LDX   $CE
400     JSR   DELAY
410     SEC
420     SBC   #$01
430     CMP   #$9F
440     BNE   DCAY
450     LDA   $1000
460     BNE   LOOP
470     BRK
480 DELAY LDY #$13
490 ROUND DEY
500     BNE   ROUND
510     DEX
520     BNE   DELAY
530     RTS
540     END
```

This may be your longest program yet. Enter and assemble it. Check the highest memory location used. Remember, we must stay between 0600 and 06FF or we will run into some memory that we shouldn't be using.

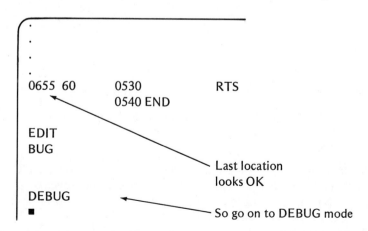

Before you execute the program, remember that you may not have entered the data to be used as the counter and the decay times. Refer to the table below, and enter the data in the Debugger mode.

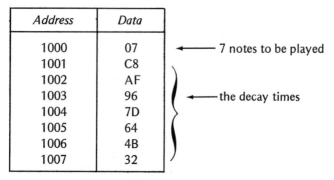

Address	Data
1000	07
1001	C8
1002	AF
1003	96
1004	7D
1005	64
1006	4B
1007	32

7 notes to be played

the decay times

Figure 12-4. Data for **Sound Shaper Program**

Now execute the program. You should be able to detect the differences in decay time.

You might want to experiment with the other parameters (attack time, peak time, frequency or volume). Feel free to modify our program to suit your own purposes.

PROGRAM TO PRINT ON THE SCREEN

Hidden away in your Atari's memory are lots of nice little subroutines that might save you much time and effort. We found one hidden away at memory location $F6A4. It will display on the screen the character whose ATASCII code is in the accumulator.

Example:

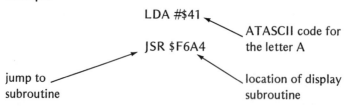

LDA #$41

ATASCII code for the letter A

JSR $F6A4

jump to subroutine

location of display subroutine

The instructions above would display the letter A, and then the cursor would move one place to the right, ready to display whatever comes next.

You must be careful when you use this subroutine if you are using the X and Y register in your program. Your values (in X and Y) will be destroyed by the subroutine as it also uses these registers. Therefore, you must make provision to save them (the stack is the ideal place for this).

The program that we will use is short, but you will have to load in lots of data in a data table. The X register and the Absolute Indexed Addressing mode will be used to load the accumulator with the ATASCII codes from the data table. The ATASCII Character Set is given in Appendix F.

PRINT ON THE SCREEN

```
100     *=$0600
110     ; PRINT ON THE SCREEN
120     LDX  #$2B      NUMBER OF CHARACTERS
130 LOOP TXA
140     PHA            SAVE NUMBER
150     LDA  $1100,X   LOAD CODE
160     JSR  $F6A4     DISPLAY CHARACTER
170     PLA            GET NUMBER BACK
180     TAX
190     DEX            COUNT DOWN
200     BNE  LOOP      GO BACK IF NOT DONE
210 LOOP1 JMP LOOP1    CIRCLE HERE
220     END
```

Enter and assemble the program. Now comes the chore of loading the data. Go into the Debugger mode and enter the data as shown.

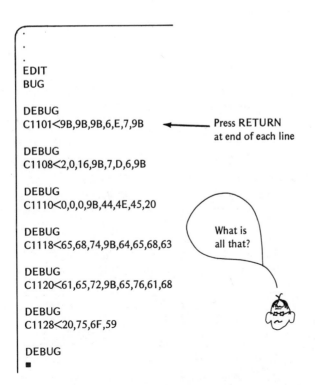

```
.
.
EDIT
BUG

DEBUG
C1101<9B,9B,9B,6,E,7,9B        ◄──────── Press RETURN
                                         at end of each line
DEBUG
C1108<2,0,16,9B,7,D,6,9B

DEBUG
C1110<0,0,0,9B,44,4E,45,20

DEBUG                              What is
C1118<65,68,74,9B,64,65,68,63     all that?

DEBUG
C1120<61,65,72,9B,65,76,61,68

DEBUG
C1128<20,75,6F,59

DEBUG
■
```

We're not going to spoil the purpose by telling you what all those numbers represent yet. If you can't wait, Figure 12-5 shows what character is represented by each code.

Before you run the program, clear the screen by holding down the | SHIFT | key and pressing the | CLEAR | key.
<

Screen is cleared

Now, execute the program by typing:

G0600   and press RETURN

This is what you see:

G0600
You have
reached
the END

The last lines of the program keep the display on the screen while the computer goes around and around doing nothing. Press the BREAK key to stop the program.

Here are the ATASCII codes used in the program.

Memory Address	Hex ATASCII Code	Character Displayed
112B	59	Y
112A	6F	o
1129	75	u
1128	20	SPACE
1127	68	h
1126	61	a
1125	76	v

1124	65	e
1123	9B	CARRIAGE RETURN
1122	72	r
1121	65	e
1120	61	a
111F	63	c
111E	68	h
111D	65	e
111C	64	d
111B	9B	CARRIAGE RETURN
111A	74	t
1119	68	h
1118	65	e
1117	20	SPACE
1116	45	E
1115	4E	N
1114	44	D
1113	9B	CARRIAGE RETURN
1112	00	♡
1111	00	♡
1110	00	♡
110F	9B	CARRIAGE RETURN
110E	06	
110D	0D	
110C	07	
110B	9B	CARRIAGE RETURN
110A	16	
1109	00	♡
1108	02	
1107	9B	CARRIAGE RETURN
1106	07	
1105	0E	
1104	06	
1103	9B	CARRIAGE RETURN
1102	9B	CARRIAGE RETURN
1101	9B	CARRIAGE RETURN

Figure 12-5. ATASCII Codes for Print on the Screen

Now, you can create your own graphics and messages by replacing our codes with any that you choose from Appendix F. You can lengthen or shorten the data table, but be sure you put the corresponding number in line 120 of the source program. Fill the screen and have fun!!

YOU'RE ON YOUR OWN

We are going to leave you at this point. You now have a fundamental knowledge of how the Assembler Cartridge works. You also have a background in the 6502 instruction set. With the understanding you now have, you can explore other assembly language features. These can be found in your Atari Assembler User's Manual. You should also explore the operation of all instructions in the 6502 set. The more that you work with assembly language programming, the more you will probably like it.

If you intend to do a sizable amount of assembly language programming, we recommend the use of the Atari 810 or 815 Disk Drive along with the Atari 820 or 822 or 825 Printer. We have used the 810 Disk Drive along with the Atari 820 printer and find them both very convenient for assembly language programming.

Good Programming!

6502 Instructions – Flags Affected

X in the box means the flag is affected. The result will depend upon the condition, or status, resulting from a previous operation. A one (1) indicates that the flag is set, a zero (0) that a flag is reset.

Mnemonic Code	Operation Performed	Status Flags							
		N	V		B	D	I	Z	C
ADC	Add memory to accumulator with carry	X	X					X	X
AND	AND memory with accumulator	X						X	
ASL	Shift left one bit (memory or accum.)	X						X	X
BCC	Branch on carry clear (If C=0)								
BCS	Branch on carry set (If C=1)								
BEQ	Branch on result zero (If Z=1)								
BIT	Test bits in accumulator with memory	X	X					X	
BMI	Branch on result minus (If N=1)								
BNE	Branch on result not zero (If Z=0)								
BPL	Branch on result plus (If N=0)								
BRK	Force break						1		
BVC	Branch on overflow clear (If V=0)								
BVS	Branch on overflow set (If V=1)								
CLC	Clear carry flag								0
CLD	Clear decimal mode					0			
CLI	Clear interrupt disable flag						0		
CLV	Clear overflow flag		0						
CMP	Compare memory and accumulator	X						X	X
CPX	Compare memory and index X	X						X	X
CPY	Compare memory and index Y	X						X	X
DEC	Decrement memory by one							X	X
DEX	Decrement index X by one							X	X
DEY	Decrement index Y by one							X	X
EOR	Exclusive OR memory with accumulator							X	X

Mnemonic Code	Operation Performed	Status Flags							
		N	V		B	D	I	Z	C
INC	Increment memory by one							X	X
INX	Increment index X by one							X	X
INY	Increment index Y by one							X	X
JMP	Jump to new location								
JSR	Jump to new location save rtn. add.								
LDA	Load accumulator from memory							X	X
LDX	Load index X from memory							X	X
LDY	Load index Y from memory							X	X
LSR	Shift right one bit (memory or accum.)	0						X	X
NOP	No operation								
ORA	OR memory with accumulator	X						X	
PHA	Push accumulator on stack								
PHP	Push processor status on stack								
PLA	Pull accumulator from stack							X	X
PLP	Pull processor status from stack	X	X	X	X	X	X	X	X
ROL	Rotate one bit left (mem. or accum.)	X						X	X
ROR	Rotate one bit right (mem. or accum.)	X						X	X
RTI	Return from interrupt	X	X	X	X	X	X	X	X
RTS	Return from subroutine								
SBC	Subtract memory and borrow from accum.	X	X					X	X
SEC	Set carry flag								1
SED	Set decimal mode					1			
SEI	Set interrupt disable flag						1		
STA	Store accumulator in memory								
STX	Store index X in memory								
STY	Store index Y in memory								
TAX	Transfer accumulator to index X	X						X	
TAY	Transfer accumulator to index Y	X						X	
TSX	Transfer stack pointer to index X	X						X	
TXA	Transfer index X to accumulator	X						X	
TXS	Transfer index X to stack pointer								
TYA	Transfer index Y to accumulator	X						X	

Flag abbreviations are:

N   Negative result flag
V   Overflow flag
    Expansion flag (not labeled)
B   Break command flag

D   Decimal mode flag
I   Interrupt disable flag
Z   Zero result flag
C   Carry flag

6502 Instructions— Addressing Modes

Mnemonic Code	Op Codes												
	Accumulator	Immediate	Zero Page	Zero Page, X	Zero Page, Y	Absolute	Absolute, X	Absolute, Y	Implied	Relative	Indexed Indirect	Indirect Indexed	Indirect
ADC	—	69	65	75	—	6D	7D	79	—	—	61	71	—
AND	—	29	25	35	—	2D	3D	39	—	—	21	31	—
ASL	0A	—	06	16	—	0E	1E	—	—	—	—	—	—
BCC	—	—	—	—	—	—	—	—	—	90	—	—	—
BCS	—	—	—	—	—	—	—	—	—	B0	—	—	—
BEQ	—	—	—	—	—	—	—	—	—	F0	—	—	—
BIT	—	—	24	—	—	2C	—	—	—	—	—	—	—
BMI	—	—	—	—	—	—	—	—	—	30	—	—	—
BNE	—	—	—	—	—	—	—	—	—	D0	—	—	—
BPL	—	—	—	—	—	—	—	—	—	10	—	—	—
BRK	—	—	—	—	—	—	—	—	00	—	—	—	—
BVC	—	—	—	—	—	—	—	—	—	50	—	—	—
BVS	—	—	—	—	—	—	—	—	—	70	—	—	—
CLC	—	—	—	—	—	—	—	—	18	—	—	—	—
CLD	—	—	—	—	—	—	—	—	D8	—	—	—	—
CLI	—	—	—	—	—	—	—	—	58	—	—	—	—
CLV	—	—	—	—	—	—	—	—	B8	—	—	—	—
CMP	—	C9	C5	D5	—	CD	DD	D9	—	—	C1	D1	—
CPX	—	E0	E4	—	—	EC	—	—	—	—	—	—	—
CPY	—	C0	C4	—	—	CC	—	—	—	—	—	—	—
DEC	—	—	C6	D6	—	CE	DE	—	—	—	—	—	—
DEX	—	—	—	—	—	—	—	—	CA	—	—	—	—
DEY	—	—	—	—	—	—	—	—	88	—	—	—	—
EOR	—	49	45	55	—	4D	5D	59	—	—.	41	51	—

Mnemonic Code	Op Codes												
	Accumulator	Immediate	Zero Page	Zero Page, X	Zero Page, Y	Absolute	Absolute, X	Absolute, Y	Implied	Relative	Indexed Indirect	Indirect Indexed	Indirect
INC	—	—	E6	F6	—	EE	FE	—	—	—	—	—	—
INX	—	—	—	—	—	—	—	—	E8	—	—	—	—
INY	—	—	—	—	—	—	—	—	C8	—	—	—	—
JMP	—	—	—	—	—	4C	—	—	—	—	—	—	6C
JSR	—	—	—	—	—	20	—	—	—	—	—	—	—
LDA	—	A9	A5	B5	—	AD	BD	B9	—	—	A1	B1	—
LDX	—	A2	A6	—	B6	AE	—	BE	—	—	—	—	—
LDY	—	A0	A4	B4	—	AC	BC	—	—	—	—	—	—
LSR	4A	—	46	56	—	4E	5E	—	—	—	—	—	—
NOP	—	—	—	—	—	—	—	—	EA	—	—	—	—
ORA	—	09	05	15	—	0D	1D	19	—	—	01	11	—
PHA	—	—	—	—	—	—	—	—	48	—	—	—	—
PHP	—	—	—	—	—	—	—	—	08	—	—	—	—
PLA	—	—	—	—	—	—	—	—	68	—	—	—	—
PLP	—	—	—	—	—	—	—	—	28	—	—	—	—
ROL	2A	—	26	36	—	2E	3E	—	—	—	—	—	—
ROR	6A	—	66	76	—	6E	7E	—	—	—	—	—	—
RTI	—	—	—	—	—	—	—	—	40	—	—	—	—
RTS	—	—	—	—	—	—	—	—	60	—	—	—	—
SBC	—	E9	E5	F5	—	ED	FD	F9	—	—	E1	F1	—
SEC	—	—	—	—	—	—	—	—	38	—	—	—	—
SED	—	—	—	—	—	—	—	—	F8	—	—	—	—
SEI	—	—	—	—	—	—	—	—	78	—	—	—	—
STA	—	—	85	95	—	8D	9D	99	—	—	81	91	—
STX	—	—	86	—	96	8E	—	—	—	—	—	—	—
STY	—	—	84	94	—	8C	—	—	—	—	—	—	—
TAX	—	—	—	—	—	—	—	—	AA	—	—	—	—
TAY	—	—	—	—	—	—	—	—	A8	—	—	—	—
TSX	—	—	—	—	—	—	—	—	BA	—	—	—	—
TXA	—	—	—	—	—	—	—	—	8A	—	—	—	—
TXS	—	—	—	—	—	—	—	—	9A	—	—	—	—
TYA	—	—	—	—	—	—	—	—	98	—	—	—	—

Frequency Values
for Three-Octave Scale

Natural Scale Note	Frequency Value	
C	1D	High
B	1F	
A#	21	
A	23	
G#	25	
G	28	
F#	2A	
F	2D	
E	2F	
D#	32	
D	35	
C#	39	
C	3C	
B	40	
A#	44	
A	48	
G#	4C	
G	51	
F#	55	
F	5B	
E	60	
D#	66	
D	6C	
C#	72	
C	79	Middle
B	80	
A#	88	
A	90	
G#	99	

Natural Scale Note	Frequency Value	
G	A2	
F#	AC	
F	B6	
E	C1	
D#	CC	
D	D9	
C#	E6	
C	F3	Low

Atari Assembler Error Codes

When an error occurs, a short "beep" is heard and the error number is displayed.

Error Number	Explanation
1	Insufficient memory for the program to be assembled.
2	The number xx cannot be found for the "DEL xx,yy" command.
3	An error in specifying an address (mini-assembler).
4	File named cannot be loaded.
5	Undefined reference label.
6	Syntax error in a statement.
7	Label defined more than once.
8	Buffer overflow.
9	No label given before "=".
10	The value of an expression is greater than 255 where one byte was required.
11	Null string used where invalid.
12	Address or address type specified is incorrect.
13	Phase error-an inconsistent result found from Pass 1 to Pass 2.
14	Undefined forward reference.
15	Line is too large.
16	Source statement not recognized by the assembler.
17	Line number too large.
18	LOMEM command was attempted after other command(s) or instruction(s). LOMEM must be first command if used.
19	No starting address given.

Atari Operating System Errors

Errors numbered above 100 refer to Operating System and Disk Operating System. Refer to DOS manual for complete list of DOS errors.

Error Number	Explanation
128	The BREAK key was hit during an I/O operation.
130	A nonexistent device was specified.
132	Command is invalid for the device selected.
136	END OF FILE READ HAS BEEN REACHED. This error may occur when reading from cassette.
137	Record was longer than 256 characters.
138	Device specified in the command does not respond. Make sure it is connected and powered.
139	Device specified in command does not return an acknowledge signal.
140	Serial framing error.
142	Serial framing error.
143	Serial data checksum error.
144	Device done error.
145	Diskette error- read-after-write comparison failed.
146	
162	Disk full.
165	File name error.

Appendix F

ATASCII Character Set

ATASCII is an abbreviation of ATARI ASCII. Letters and numbers have the same values as those in ASCII, but some of the special characters have been assigned differently. Characters 80-FF (hex) are just reverse colors of 1-7F except for the characters shown (9B-9F and FD, FE, and FF).

HEX	CHARACTER	HEX	CHARACTER	HEX	CHARACTER
0		A		14	
1		B		15	
2		C		16	
3		D		17	
4		E		18	
5		F		19	
6		10		1A	
7		11		1B	
8		12		1C	
9		13		1D	

HEX	CHARACTER	HEX	CHARACTER	HEX	CHARACTER
1E	←	32	2	46	F
1F	→	33	3	47	G
20	Space	34	4	48	H
21	!	35	5	49	I
22	"	36	6	4A	J
23	#	37	7	4B	K
24	$	38	8	4C	L
25	%	39	9	4D	M
26	&	3A	:	4E	N
27	'	3B	;	4F	O
28	(	3C	<	50	P
29	)	3D	=	51	Q
2A	*	3E	>	52	R
2B	+	3F	?	53	S
2C	,	40	@	54	T
2D	-	41	A	55	U
2E	.	42	B	56	V
2F	/	43	C	57	W
30	0	44	D	58	X
31	1	45	E	59	Y

HEX	CHARACTER	HEX	CHARACTER	HEX	CHARACTER
5A	Z	6A	j	7A	z
5B	[	6B	k	7B	[graphic]
5C	\	6C	l	7C	[up arrow]
5D	]	6D	m	7D	[graphic]
5E	^	6E	n	7E	[graphic]
5F	—	6F	o	7F	[graphic]
60	[graphic]	70	p	9B	Carriage Return
61	a	71	q	9C	[graphic]
62	b	72	r	9D	[graphic]
63	c	73	s	9E	[graphic]
64	d	74	t	9F	[graphic]
65	e	75	u	FD	[graphic] (Buzzer)
66	f	76	v	FE	[graphic] Delete character
67	g	77	w	FF	[graphic] Insert character
68	h	78	x		
69	i	79	y		

Index